PREPARING FOR THE INFORMATION AGE

Synoptic Report of the Education Departments'
Superhighways Initiative

WELSH OFFICE	DEPARTMENT OF EDUCATION NORTHERN IRELAND	THE SCOTTISH OFFICE	DEPARTMENT FOR EDUCATION AND EMPLOYMENT

Welsh Office
Y Swyddfa Gymreig

DENI
DEPARTMENT OF EDUCATION
NORTHERN IRELAND

THE SCOTTISH OFFICE

D*f*EE

Foreword
Dr Kim Howells, MP

The Education Departments' Superhighways Initiative, or EDSI, was launched in 1995. Since then it has gathered strength, culminating in 25 different projects taking part and involving over 1,000 schools and colleges across the whole of the UK. Partnership with commercial enterprise, which largely funded the projects, has been particularly welcome.

EDSI has an important part to play in informing our approach to the challenges of the Information Age. Not the least of these challenges face the education service. ICT literacy is a key skill in today's world, alongside literacy and numeracy. In the last 20 years, new technology has revolutionised the workplace. We must now ensure that our education system provides Britain's children with the tools they need as adults in tomorrow's economy and society. We intend to transform education in Britain, to bring it to the level of the best in the world, and to enhance our competitiveness and quality of life. We are determined that the opportunities offered by new technologies will not pass our education system by, and that the benefits should be available to all, including those with special and individual needs.

That is why the Government - in partnership with private enterprise - has funded the independent evaluation of these projects and the dissemination of the results. We wish as many people as possible to gain from the experience of project participants. We are now looking carefully at the EDSI outcomes and considering how best to use them to underpin our new plans for the National Grid for Learning.

The Grid will build on the experiences of other initiatives, such as EDSI. It will provide curriculum support for schools and help teacher development, and will extend to lifelong learning, whether home-based learning, further education or training for employment. It will link closely with our plans for study centres funded through the National Lottery and for the University for Industry. National and local museums and galleries will have an important part to play. We also intend that libraries will be an integral part of the Grid. In this way we will be able to make available to all learners the riches of the world's intellectual, cultural and scientific heritage.

Through the Grid, we will:

- **train teachers,** to ensure that all teachers are ICT-literate

- **connect schools** and keep access charges as low as possible

- **provide content,** developing plans for a public/private partnership to deliver educational software and services to teachers, pupils and other learners

- **remove barriers** to learning, ensuring equality of access for all, including those in isolated rural areas, those with special educational needs or those in areas of urban deprivation.

It is encouraging to see from this report how much progress has been made to date in using information and communication technologies for learning benefits. That so much progress has been made in so short a time is a tribute to the schools and colleges who took part; and to their partners in industry who helped to frame project proposals and to fund them. I have also been impressed by the hard work of the evaluation teams and the synoptic evaluator, who have jointly drawn out the learning points for all of us from the projects. The future for the education service looks very promising.

Contents

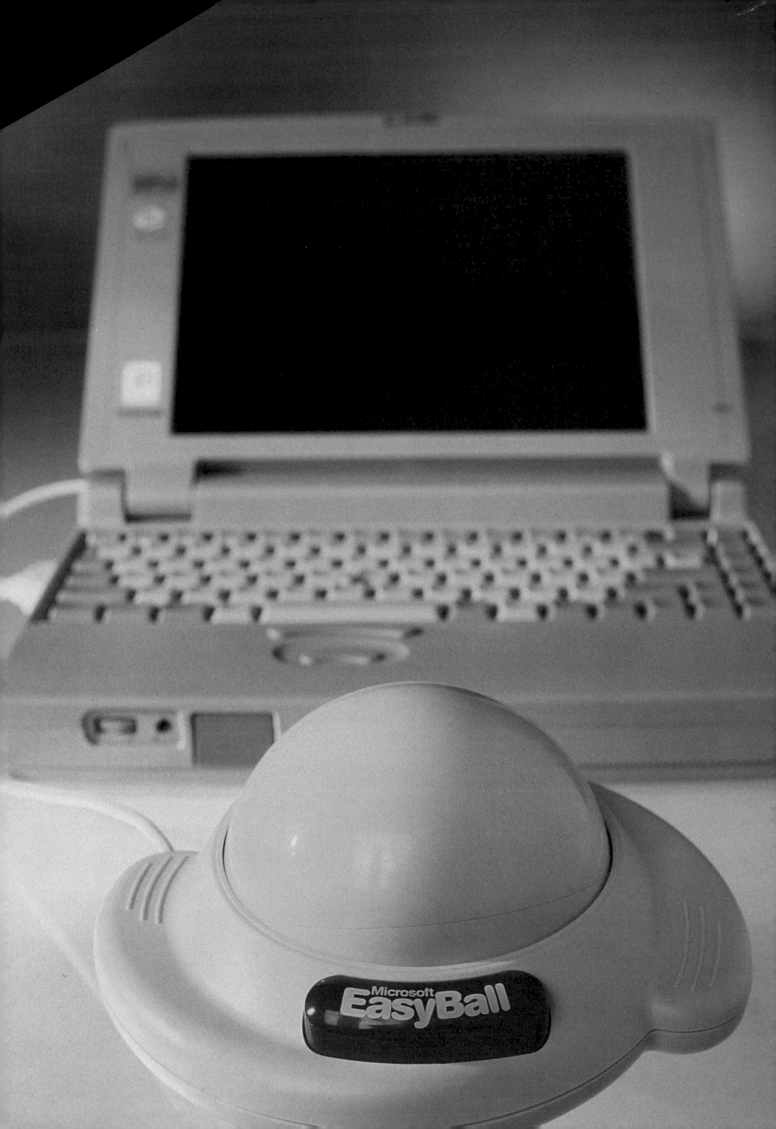

Section 1
Executive Summary

1. The Education Departments' Superhighways Initiative (EDSI) was set up jointly by the then Secretaries of State for Education and Employment, and for Scotland, Wales and Northern Ireland. EDSI was launched in autumn 1995, with the majority of projects running until early summer 1997. The initiative eventually comprised 25 pilot projects, some containing distinct sub-projects. Largely based in the school and further education college sectors, the projects were proposed and funded jointly by educational institutions and commercial companies, with the Government funding a set of independent evaluations.

2. The projects fell into two broad categories: those directed mainly at using information and communications technology (ICT) to support learners in schools and colleges, and those directed at supporting professional development and training. The former can be further divided into those primarily concerned with vocational training, home-school links and the school curriculum more generally.

3. The aim of the Initiative was to look at ways in which schools and colleges might use the emerging information superhighway to contribute to learning. More specifically, the project evaluators considered three questions:

   • Which forms of ICT produce benefits that directly or indirectly improve learning?

   • What conditions are needed in a given school or college to enable these benefits to be achieved?

   • What infrastructure is needed (locally and nationally) to ensure steady and continuous improvement both in ICT and in the capacity of all schools and colleges to make good use of it?

4. The overall level of staff enthusiasm for, and experience of, IT in the schools and colleges volunteering to take part in the EDSI projects was probably above average, but nearly all of the projects also included numbers of institutions with fairly modest prior IT experience or provision. Statistical extrapolations from project schools and colleges to UK schools and colleges as a whole are not possible, as the EDSI participants are unlikely to be representative. Implementation delays curtailed the time available for classroom evaluation. However, within these constraints, the evaluations do indicate what qualitative effects the projects had on institutions at various stages of development in terms of their educational use of IT. The method of analysis used in this report is therefore based on identifying the factors which influenced what was learned, how teachers handled the challenges which the technologies presented, and the ways in which the organisation of ICT activities by the project partners affected what happened in the classroom.

5. The evaluators' executive summaries suggest that they judged 12 of the the projects and sub-projects to have achieved their initial objectives more or less fully, while six achieved them to some extent, and five did not achieve them – or only to a limited extent. Most of the remainder were projects that entered the programme at a later date, and so were not complete at the time of writing.

6. Each EDSI project introduced some combination of three kinds of ICT activities for learners, namely:

   • **accessing resources held elsewhere**
   (using the Internet, CD-ROM resources held elsewhere, cable TV or interactive TV)

   • **creating resources for access by others**
   (through the Internet, CD-ROM or interactive TV)

   • **electronic communication**
   (using e-mail, fax, text-based discussion, text-based conferencing and video conferencing).

7. Most projects tried out more than one system, and some included several. The evaluations indicated that there were real possibilities for improving learning through the use of ICT, and that virtually all the technologies used had educational value. However, what this value was, and how it could best be realised, appeared to vary significantly from one technology to another.

Benefits for learning

8. Six main effects on learning were reported, several of them extending across a number of classrooms in a variety of projects:

   • improved subject learning

   • the development of network literacy

   • improved vocational training

   • improved motivation and attitudes to learning

   • the development of independent learning and research skills

   • social development.

   Of these, the first two need some further comment.

9. Network literacy may be defined as the capacity to use electronic networks to access resources, to create resources, and to communicate with others. These three elements of network literacy can be seen as complex extensions of the traditional skills of reading, writing, speaking and listening. The

notion also extends previous conceptions of IT literacy, which conventionally involve interactions with and around the computer. To this we must now add interactions at a distance through ICT.

10. Improved subject learning has been reported across a wide range of curriculum areas. These have included English, mathematics, science, history, geography, modern languages, Welsh, art, technology, IT and careers, as well as independent study and cross-curricular project work. ICT systems appear to be useable in some form across the full age range, from infants to adults, although for several kinds of system the projects did not cover all age ranges.

11. There has been little indication of differential access or learning effects by gender or ethnic group. However, special needs learners have gained proportionately more than others from access to ICT, especially in terms of motivation and self-confidence. Examples of successful provision for special needs learners of different ages included:

- an FE college providing electronic distance tutoring for severely physically disabled adults

- hearing-impaired secondary school students communicating with each other by using video conferencing

- secondary school students with behavioural problems using video conferencing to improve their conversation and listening skills, self presentation and confidence

- able children in very small rural primary schools gaining considerably in motivation from inter-school project work involving e-mail and text-based conferencing.

12. One area where there are serious questions of equity and access to ICT-based learning concerns children in small rural schools, where the provision of broadband networked services may be less commercially attractive than in schools serving more heavily populated areas.

13. Schools and colleges used ICT to pursue a range of indirect benefits in addition to the learning benefits themselves. These included:

- increasing the institution's curriculum resources

- promoting staff development

- improving management and administration

- retaining current learners and gaining new ones

- increasing the institution's physical and financial resources

- increasing the human resources available to the institution without taking on additional paid staff

- obtaining publicity to raise the standing of the institution.

14. Each of these different benefits took a wide variety of forms, as schools and colleges explored ways of using different combinations of ICT systems for their own purposes. Improvements in management and administration, for example, included:

- teachers accessing the school server from home for record keeping and administration

- using ICT to reduce the cost of administrative communications with an education authority

- improving communications over such matters as pupil transfer

- employing ICT to support training in educational management and administration

- teachers using laptop computers at home and at work for

school reports or for exam administration.

15. Several factors affected the benefits a given project school or college gained:

- quality of management

- quality of the other project partners

- stance towards IT generally

- current and anticipated levels of financial and physical resources available and required, in addition to those provided by the project

- quality of the new technologies that the project made available

- dominant educational and social philosophy

- match between the technologies available and the circumstances and priorities of the school or college.

Training implications of ICT

16. Training teachers to make effective use of entirely new systems presented a number of challenges, but after some initial setbacks most projects found ways of providing suitable training programmes for staff and others involved. A number of conclusions emerged from their experiences.

17. The central importance of both initial and continuing training needs to be recognised and budgeted for from the outset. Teachers need to know not only how to operate the systems in a technical sense, but also what educational possibilities they have, and the consequences of their introduction both for teaching strategies and for curriculum planning. The educational and technical aspects need to be developed together; training provided by combining ICT systems and face-to-face interaction was used successfully in several teams to achieve this.

18. Education authorities will need to revise current support and training provision to take account of ICT. They will also need to prepare for a future in which schools can use ICT to obtain INSET courses (including tutorial elements through video conferencing and e-mail) from distant providers. The possibilities here for national and regional specialisation and the creation of consortia of training providers are considerable, but a national lead will be necessary to ensure that the best use is made of the limited number of ICT trainers with school experience.

19. The national requirements for initial teacher education and for continuing professional development will need to take account of the introduction of ICT, as will the content of the various national curricula.

Partnership between business, government and education

20. The EDSI concept of an ICT partnership between business, local and national government and education has, after some initial hesitations and difficulties, proved its worth, although much remains to be done to strengthen these links.

ICT readiness

21. What is now needed is to find ways of improving further the schools, colleges, technologies and supporting infrastructure, through a steady, planned and sustained programme of research, selective development and dissemination. This will involve drawing clear distinctions between technologies already suitable for universal use, those suitable only for particularly experienced schools and colleges, and those that are at this stage still experimental.

22. In the educational context, any ICT technology intended for universal take-up needs to be:

    - demonstrably educationally valuable

    - widely available

    - affordable

    - reliable

    - technically supportable

    - useable by any appropriate teacher and any appropriate learner.

23. The EDSI technologies can be provisionally classified as:

    - **established technologies** ready for universal take-up; these are fax, e-mail, text-based conferencing, Internet sites (where these are used for accessing resources) and CD-ROMs

    - **useable technologies** already of demonstrable value and useable in favourable situations, where cost permits; these are Web pages and sites (where these are being produced by learners), the open integrated learning system used in EDSI, and video conferencing

    - **experimental technologies** worth further investigation, but whose educational value is not yet established; these are text-based discussion and interactive TV (iTV).

24. The classification of a given technology will change over time and new technologies will continue to appear, so arrangements are needed to ensure that technological developments are routinely encouraged, trialled, evaluated and considered for universal adoption on a systematic basis.

25. Schools and colleges, too, are at various stages of readiness. The first task here is to identify formally those institutions that are ready to benefit from full ICT development, and to ensure that they can introduce and expand access to established forms of ICT.

26. At the same time, institutions that are not yet ready to benefit from full ICT development will need advice, support and encouragement to enable them to become so.

Support: resources, mechanisms and infrastructure

27. Given that the level of success achieved by project schools and colleges was in part a function of the support and resources that the project teams provided, an equivalent local infrastructure would be required. However, there would also need to be a regional and national infrastructure.

28. Within the local infrastructure, mechanisms would be needed to:

    - organise the grouping of all schools into neighbourhood clusters

    - provide support for clusters at education authority level

    - encourage and support links between the schools and other local partners, such as parents, business, libraries and colleges

    - arrange the provision (either at cluster or education authority level) of a managed service for the physical network

    - ensure local availability of key categories of ICT staff

    - assist ICT companies in identifying suitable schools and colleges for the further trialling and improvement of experimental and useable, but not yet established, technologies.

29. National and regional mechanisms would be needed to:

- identify schools ready to benefit from full ICT development

- agree an overall policy for linking funding from different sources to the ICT development programme

- provide a coherent set of national Internet sites to support different groups of teachers and other staff by establishing a one-stop shop for obtaining information and contacts to assist with professional and curriculum development issues

- ensure that relevant changes were made to national curricula, initial teacher training and continuing professional development

- systematically review each useable technology with a view to its being upgraded to the status of an established technology

- systematically monitor developments in experimental technologies world-wide, with a view to developing suitable technologies into useable forms in the UK.

30. As each technology reached 'established' status, it would – given the availability of adequate funding – become the subject of national dissemination and support. This would involve:

- making the technologies available to all schools and colleges demonstrably ready and willing to take them

- simultaneous provision of targeted INSET support for staff in those schools and colleges

- inclusion of the use of that technology in relevant forms of continuing professional development and in initial teacher training, and a review of any implications for the various national curricula.

31. How present organisations and procedures would need to be adjusted to create this sort of infrastructure and programme goes beyond the scope of this report, but some comment on resources is appropriate.

32. The provision of secure long-term resources to develop the programme is a central issue, partly though not exclusively a matter of funding. Schools and colleges can use the introduction of ICT as a way of generating additional resources of many kinds from the local community and beyond. Virtually all these ways of increasing resources offer indirect benefits for current or future learners, and represent an important driving force for institutional growth and community development.

33. Opportunities for different schools and colleges to gain access to several of these kinds of resource are, unfortunately, often unequal. In general, smaller schools with younger learners – especially in poorer or more sparsely populated areas – are likely to receive less funding per learner.

34. The popularity of ICT may draw learners and private sector resources disproportionately towards the schools that are best placed to fund and further develop their existing ICT provision. If this seriously de-stabilises other schools nearby, the resources that should have gone into developing the ICT capabilities of those schools may instead have to provide basic emergency support.

35. More could be done to encourage schools and colleges to increase the proportion of internal funding they allocate to ICT, but this alone is unlikely to be enough to cover the introduction of ICT. Nor will the additional resources created by

involving parents and local companies, or by attracting more people back into education, cover the cost of introducing networks and systems into schools and colleges. Such developments pre-suppose equipment and trained, enthusiastic staff: they do not precede it. The benefits of ICT can feed the further growth of schools and colleges once they are started on the development process, but they are not themselves a starting point.

36. While the Initiative has had considerable success drawing in the ICT companies to act as funders and providers of support, only a relatively small percentage of schools and colleges participated in EDSI. It is hard to see how the ICT industry could assume responsibility for funding the remainder at the same level, although it certainly has a continuing contribution to make in research and product development, and by setting education prices and tariffs at reasonable levels.

37. Clearly, schools will need assistance if they are to become well informed customers for ICT systems and support: the good-practice and decision-making guide being prepared by NCET, based in part on the work of the evaluators, should help with this. It will also be important for schools and colleges to review the priority they are giving to new technologies in terms of resourcing, and for there to be seedcorn funding available from Government to help set these developments in motion within each school and college.

Meeting the challenge

38. Across the EDSI projects, a clear pattern has emerged. The introduction of ICT overcomes or blurs many different boundaries, including those between subjects, between the academic and the social

aspects of a topic or problem, between learners of different ages and abilities, between different categories of teachers, between teachers and other adults as co-workers in supporting learners, between home and school, between school and work, and between schools and colleges. These technologies also have the capacity to dissolve some of the distinctions between the local neighbourhood and places far away, and between face-to-face and remote communication.

39. While few of these effects are entirely new, what is new is that the same set of technologies can produce them all, and in a stronger and increasingly more convergent form than in the past. Furthermore, the technological complexities of ICT systems are substantial, so the managerial and organisational demands made on all those introducing them will be considerable.

40. Establishing a national development programme will undoubtedly be extremely challenging. However, the new technologies provide exciting opportunities for those who are willing to help create a learning society open to all. Whether all those involved are prepared to make the commitments needed to take up the challenge is now the central issue.

Section 2
Main Report

1. There is widespread agreement that in future the UK must become a society in which creating and disseminating knowledge plays a central role. From one perspective, these activities form the core of many of our most creative industries. From another perspective, to gain knowledge is, in a modern society, a precondition for national success and many aspects of individual fulfilment. A society wishing to empower all its members to realise their individual and collective aspirations will have to become a society in which lifelong learning is available to all.

2. The convergence of information technology and communications may well help to create such a society. The various information and communications technology (ICT) systems and networks now available are rapidly evolving to form part of an international information superhighway. This potentially offers most people in the developed world a means of creating and disseminating information world-wide at low cost, and new ways of communicating with individuals and groups around the world.

3. Building a learning society of this kind will involve co-operation between many kinds of organisation, including higher education, businesses, libraries, voluntary organisations, the media and local and national government. The Education Departments' Superhighways Initiative (EDSI) dealt with one important part of this task by looking at ways in which schools and colleges might use the emerging information superhighway to contribute to this development.

4. EDSI was launched at a national conference in November 1995 and ran to early summer 1997. It was set up jointly by the then Secretaries of State for Education and Employment, and for Scotland, Wales and Northern Ireland. It initially comprised 23 pilot projects, largely based in the school and further education (FE) sectors, but including two involving higher education (HE). These were proposed and funded jointly by educational institutions and commercial companies, with the Government funding a set of independent evaluations. One of the original projects was withdrawn and another three added, giving 25 in all. Two of the projects had distinct sub-projects within them; these sub-projects are generally treated separately in what follows. Brief details of all the projects are given in the executive summaries of the evaluations, which can be found in the appendices to this report.

5. The EDSI projects fell into two broad categories: those directed mainly at using ICT to support learners in schools and colleges, and those directed at supporting professional

Table 1 Number of schools and colleges in each project (Autumn Term 1996)

	Primary schools	Secondary schools	Special schools	FE colleges	HE insti-tutions	Homes	Total
Acorn Home-School Links Project	8	2	0	0	1	92	103
Birmingham Knowledge Superhighways Project	0	6	0	0	0	0	6
Bristol Education On-Line Network Project (BEON)	9	1	1	0	0	0	11
Burnley LIFE Programme (Learning via Interactive and Flexible Education)	0	8	1	0	0	0	9
CLASS Project	0	4	0	0	0	0	4
Cumbria Broadband Pilot: Carlisle Schools Video-Conferencing Project	0	3	0	0	0	0	3
Cumbria Broadband Pilot: Furness Highway Project	0	8	2	2	0	0	12
Dyfed Satellite Project: Opening the Door to Satellite Remote Sensing	0	16	0	0	0	0	16
Educational Internet Service Providers Project (EISP)	21	29	4	0	0	0	54
GEMISIS 2000 Schools Project	0	2	0	0	0	0	2
Hertfordshire: 'Students as Writers' Project	2	2	0	0	0	0	4
Hertfordshire: Link Centre at Queens' School, Bushey	0	1	0	0	0	0	1
Highdown Information Hub Project	0	3	0	0	0	53	56
Journeys through Space and Time (now called Rosendale Odyssey)	1	0	0	0	0	0	1
Kent Broadband Learning Project	1	2	0	0	0	0	3
Lingu@NET – a Virtual Language Centre	Not applicable						
Live-Links Project for Surgical Training	0	0	0	0	5	0	5
London Colleges Multimedia Initiative	0	0	0	22	0	0	22
Modern Communications for Teaching and Learning in Argyll and Bute	88	10	0	0	0	0	98
Multimedia Portables for Teachers Pilot	77	474	16	0	0	0	567
Powys Access for Schools Project (PACCS)	3	1	1	0	0	0	5
Project ConnectEd (also known as Project IntraNet)	0	20	0	0	0	0	20
Students Across Europe Project	0	3	0	0	0	0	3
Superhighways in Education Project	0	3	0	0	0	0	3
Superhighways Teams Across Rural Schools (STARS)	16	0	0	0	0	0	16
Teachers Managing Learning Project	137	15	3	0	0	0	155
Virtual Workplace Project (formerly Broadband Support for GNVQ IT Courses)	0	0	0	3	1	0	4
Total	363	613	28	27	7	145	1,183

Note: Covers total of 25 projects, two of which had two sub-projects

development and training. Of these, the former can be further divided into those primarily concerned with vocational training, home-school links and the school curriculum more generally. Projects differed greatly in size (see Table 1) and in the curriculum areas and educational issues they set out to explore.

6. The EDSI projects were evaluated by teams from: the University of Leicester and the University College of Wales, Aberystwyth; the Scottish Council for Research in Education; the University of Leeds; Homerton College, Cambridge and Magee College, University of Ulster; Lancaster University; the Joint Centre for Education in Medicine and the Open University; the University of Warwick, NCET and the University of Nottingham. Full evaluation reports (available on the World Wide Web at http://www.ncet.org.uk/edsi) were prepared on the original 22 projects, and unpublished interim reports were available for the others. The reports collectively provide a rich and informative analysis of what has been achieved, which no synopsis can hope to match. This present interpretation should therefore be read within the framework of the substantive reports.

7. By late 1996 the Initiative involved over 1,000 schools and 27 colleges. As involvement was by application (and not all projects proposed were accepted), the project schools and colleges are untypical of schools and colleges nationally in significant, but generally unquantifiable, ways – although primary schools are clearly under-represented.

8. The evaluators' executive summaries indicate that they judged that 12 projects and sub-projects achieved their initial objectives more or less fully, six achieved them to some extent and five achieved them only to a limited extent or not at all. The remaining few were mainly projects that entered the programme at a later date, and so were not complete at the time of writing this synoptic report. It should be emphasised that, as might be expected with exploratory pilot schemes, virtually all the projects changed quite radically during the period of the evaluation, and some schools and commercial sponsors left or joined projects over the evaluation period. A number of projects were renamed. The projects and their evaluators are listed in Table 2.

9. It is highly probable that the overall level of enthusiasm for, and experience of, IT in project schools and colleges was above average, but

Table 2   Projects and their evaluation teams

Group A Evaluated by University of Leicester and University College of Wales, Aberystwyth	Curriculum Projects in England and Wales
	A2.1 Bristol Education On-Line Network Project (BEON)
	A2.2 Project ConnectEd (also known as Project IntraNet)
	A2.3 Kent Broadband Learning Project
	A2.4 Birmingham Knowledge Superhighways Project
	A2.5 Journeys through Space and Time (now called Rosendale Odyssey)
	A2.6 Dyfed Satellite Project – Opening the Door to Satellite Remote Sensing
	A2.7 Powys Access for Schools Project (PACCS)
Group S Evaluated by The Scottish Council for Research in Education	**Curriculum Projects in Scotland**
	S2.1 Modern Communications for Teaching and Learning in Argyll and Bute
	S2.2 Superhighways Teams Across Rural Schools (STARS)
Group B Evaluated by University of Leeds	**Vocationally-Focused Projects**
	B2.1 Virtual Workplace Project (formerly named Broadband Support for GNVQ IT Courses)
	B2.2 Students Across Europe Project
	B2.3 GEMISIS 2000 Schools Project
	B2.4 Burnley LIFE Programme (Learning via Interactive and Flexible Education)
	B2.5 London Colleges Multimedia Initiative
	Cumbria Broadband Pilot:
	B2.6 Carlisle Schools Video-Conferencing Project
	B2.7 Furness Highway Project
	Hertfordshire:
	B2.8 'Students as Writers' Project
	B2.9 Link Centre at Queens' School, Bushey
Group C Evaluated by Homerton College, Cambridge, and Magee College, University of Ulster	**Teachers' Professional Development**
	C2.1 CLASS Project
	C2.2 Teachers Managing Learning Project
Group D Evaluated by Lancaster University	**Home-School Links**
	D2.1 Acorn Home-School Links Project
	D2.2 Highdown Information Hub Project
	D2.3 Superhighways in Education Project
Group E Evaluated by Joint Centre for Education in Medicine and the Open University	**Higher and Professional Education**
	E2.1 Live-Links Project for Surgical Training
Group F Evaluated by University of Warwick, NCET and University of Nottingham	**Additional Projects**
	F2.1 Educational Internet Service Providers Project (EISP)
	F2.2 Lingu@NET Project
	F2.3 Multimedia Portables for Teachers Pilot

Note: For information about the referencing system and about how to access the full reports on the Web, see pages 47, 48 and 49

nearly all of the projects also included some institutions with fairly modest prior IT experience or provision. While statistical extrapolations from project schools and colleges to UK schools and colleges as a whole were not possible, the evaluations indicate the qualitative effects which the projects had on institutions at various stages of development in terms of their educational use of IT. The method of analysis used in this report is therefore based upon identifying the factors which influenced what was learned, how teachers handled the challenges the technologies presented, and in what ways the organisation of ICT activities by the project partners affected what happened in the classroom.

10. The projects varied greatly in the ICT systems they used. It was also notable that projects tended to involve more than one system (see Table 3).

11. How projects used these systems to organise their ICT-based activities at classroom level and with what results will be discussed below, but it is clear that, for most schools and colleges, setting up the projects and creating support structures for them were time-consuming pre-conditions for successful classroom use. Most of the rest of this report will therefore consider in turn the following three questions.

- Which forms of ICT produce benefits that directly or indirectly improve learning?

- What conditions are needed in a given school or college to enable these benefits to be achieved?

- What infrastructure, support, software and services are needed (locally and nationally) to ensure steady and continuous improvement both in ICT and also in the capacity of all schools and colleges to make good use of it?

12. Subsequent parts of the report consider how the EDSI findings relate to these questions, before drawing together the strands to identify the recommendations emerging for future policy.

Developing the individual learner: classrooms, teaching and lifelong learning

13. The central thrust of the Initiative was to find ways of using ICT to develop the capability of individual

Table 3   ICT systems used in each project

	Internet	Video conferencing	E-mail	CD-ROM	Digital camera	OILS	Text-based discussion	Text-based conferencing	Fax	Cable TV	iTV	TOTAL
Acorn Home-School Links Project	1										1	2
Birmingham Knowledge Superhighways Project	1	1	1			1						4
Bristol Education On-Line Network Project (BEON)	1	1	1	1	1	1						6
Burnley LIFE Programme (Learning via Interactive and Flexible Education)	1	1										2
CLASS Project		1		1								2
Cumbria Broadband Pilot: Carlisle Schools Video-Conferencing Project		1										1
Cumbria Broadband Pilot: Furness Highway Project	1	1	1						1			4
Dyfed Satellite Project: Opening the Door to Satellite Remote Sensing	1	1										2
Educational Internet Service Providers Project (EISP)	1		1									2
GEMISIS 2000 Schools Project	1	1	1	1		1						5
Hertfordshire: 'Students as Writers' Project	1		1									2
Hertfordshire: Link Centre at Queens' School, Bushey				1								1
Highdown Information Hub Project	1		1	1								3
Journeys through Space and Time (now called Rosendale Odyssey)	1		1		1							3
Kent Broadband Learning Project	1	1	1	1						1		5
Lingu@NET – a Virtual Language Centre	1		1									2
Live-Links Project for Surgical Training		1										1
London Colleges Multimedia Initiative	1	1	1	1	1							5
Modern Communications for Teaching and Learning in Argyll and Bute		1	1					1	1			4
Multimedia Portables for Teachers Pilot	1			1								2
Powys Access for Schools Project (PACCS)	1	1	1									3
Project ConnectEd (also known as Project IntraNet)	1	1	1		1		1					5
Students Across Europe Project		1										1
Superhighways in Education Project	1	1	1	1						1		5
Superhighways Teams Across Rural Schools (STARS)	1						1	1				3
Teachers Managing Learning Project	1	1							1			3
Virtual Workplace Project (formerly Broadband Support for GNVQ IT Courses)				1								1
TOTAL	20	17	15	10	4	3	2	2	3	2	1	

Note: Covers total of 25 projects, two of which had two sub-projects

learners. To do this, one or more of three main kinds of ICT-based activities were introduced, namely:

- accessing resources held elsewhere (using the Internet, resources on CD-ROM held elsewhere, cable TV or interactive TV)

- creating resources for access by others (via the Internet, CD-ROM or interactive TV)

- electronic communication (using fax, e-mail, text-based conferencing, text-based discussion and video conferencing).

14. These activities were spread differentially across projects (see Table 4), with accessing resources and communication receiving the greatest emphasis.

Benefits for learners

15. The learning benefits reported by the evaluators can be grouped into six main categories:

- improved subject learning

- development of network literacy

- improved vocational training

- improved motivation and attitudes to learning

- development of independent learning and research skills

- social development.

16. Many of these benefits were common to a number of classrooms and emerged in many projects (see Table 5).

17. Network literacy may be defined as the capacity to use electronic networks to access resources, to create resources and to communicate with others. These three elements can be seen as complex extensions of the traditional skills of reading, writing, speaking and listening. The notion extends previous conceptions of IT literacy, which conventionally involves

interactions with and around the computer. To this we must now add interactions at a distance through ICT.

18. In one sense, all of the projects that made any progress must have promoted some elements of network literacy as a result; however, the effect is included in Table 5 only where the evaluation team noted it specifically.

19. The school-related projects between them covered almost all curriculum subjects. In some cases, subject learning was accompanied by improvements in independent learning and research skills. FE colleges have far more diverse curricula to deal with, so curriculum coverage here was proportionately less – especially in the area of vocational courses. However, where vocational training was a project objective, it was generally achieved to some extent.

Table 4 Learning activities arising in each project

	Accessing resources elsewhere	Creating resources for others	Electronic communication
Acorn Home-School Links Project	2	2	1
Birmingham Knowledge Superhighways Project	1		2
Bristol Education On-Line Network Project (BEON)	2	1	2
Burnley LIFE Programme (Learning via Interactive and Flexible Education)	1	1	2
Cumbria Broadband Pilot: Carlisle Schools Video-Conferencing Project			2
Cumbria Broadband Pilot: Furness Highway Project	2	1	2
Dyfed Satellite Project: Opening the Door to Satellite Remote Sensing	2		2
Educational Internet Service Providers Project (EISP)	2	1	2
GEMISIS 2000 Schools Project	2		2
Hertfordshire: 'Students as Writers' Project	1		2
Hertfordshire: Link Centre at Queens' School, Bushey	2		
Highdown Information Hub Project	2	2	1
Journeys through Space and Time (now called Rosendale Odyssey)		2	1
Kent Broadband Learning Project	2	1	2
London Colleges Multimedia Initiative	2	2	2
Modern Communications for Teaching and Learning in Argyll and Bute	2		2
Powys Access for Schools Project (PACCS)	1	1	2
Project ConnectEd (also known as Project IntraNet)	1	1	1
Students Across Europe Project			2
Superhighways in Education Project	2		2
Superhighways Teams Across Rural Schools (STARS)	1		2
Virtual Workplace Project (formerly Broadband Support for GNVQ IT Courses)	too early to judge		
TOTAL	30	15	36

Note 1: 2 = major emphasis within project; 1 = minor emphasis within project

Note 2: Professional development projects excluded

Table 5 Main reported learning effects, by project

	Development of network literacy	Improved subject learning	Improved vocational training	Improved motivation and attitudes	Independent learning and research skills	Social development
Acorn Home-School Links Project				1		
Birmingham Knowledge Superhighways Project		1	1	1	1	1
Bristol Education On-Line Network Project (BEON)	1	1		1	1	1
Burnley LIFE Programme (Learning via Interactive and Flexible Education)	1		1	1		
Cumbria Broadband Pilot: Carlisle Schools Video-Conferencing Project	1	1				
Cumbria Broadband Pilot: Furness Highway Project	1	1		1		
Dyfed Satellite Project: Opening the Door to Satellite Remote Sensing	1	1		1		1
Educational Internet Service Providers Project (EISP)	1	1	1	1	1	1
GEMISIS 2000 Schools Project	1					
Hertfordshire: 'Students as Writers' Project	Too early to judge					
Hertfordshire: Link Centre at Queens' School, Bushey		1		1		
Highdown Information Hub Project	1	1		1	1	1
Journeys through Space and Time (now called Rosendale Odyssey)		1		1		1
Kent Broadband Learning Project	1	1		1	1	1
London Colleges Multimedia Initiative	1	1	1	1		
Modern Communications for Teaching and Learning in Argyll and Bute	1	1		1	1	
Powys Access for Schools Project (PACCS)		1	1		1	
Project ConnectEd (also known as Project IntraNet)	1	1	1	1	1	1
Students Across Europe Project		1		1		1
Superhighways in Education Project		1		1	1	
Superhighways Teams Across Rural Schools (STARS)				1	1	1
Virtual Workplace Project (formerly Broadband Support for GNVQ IT Courses)	Too early to judge					
TOTAL	12	17	6	17	10	10

Note 1: Professional development projects excluded

Note 2: EISP entries provisional, as project not yet completed

20. The most frequently reported learning benefits were improvements in motivation and attitudes to learning. This was found in virtually all projects that made enough progress towards classroom implementation for the question to arise. It should be emphasised, however, that where a learning benefit occurred within a project, it was seldom, if ever, a benefit gained by every learner, nor did it occur within every participating school or college. As will emerge later, institutional and classroom factors were major influences upon success levels.

21. In general, there has been little indication of differential access to learning by gender or ethnic group (S3.46, D3.37, A3.67). However, special needs learners appear to have gained more than others from access to ICT. These benefits were gained through a variety of kinds of ICT provision, and across a number of different contexts and age ranges.

• In one case, an FE college in London provided electronic distance tutoring (using European Union funding) for 14 severely physically disabled adults, with each programme catering for the individual's specific disabilities. PCs were provided for home use, and a weekly tutorial visit to each student's home was organised to supplement their college attendances (B2.5.45).

• In other colleges, video conferencing was used to allow hearing-impaired students to communicate with each other through signing, whiteboarding and text talk (B3.21). An interesting variant of this approach, this time in a secondary school, was demonstrated by another hearing-impaired student who would not speak at all in school, but who was able to do so over a video-conferencing link to a student who was visually impaired (A2.6.70).

• Video conferencing was successful with secondary students with behavioural problems, who used it to improve their conversation and listening skills, self presentation and confidence. For a number of these learners, the video conferencing – far from increasing the difficulty of talking with others – appears to reduce this difficulty. The new confidence thus gained was, in this case at least, later transferred to face-to-face situations (A3.67-69).

• Able children in small rural primary schools gained considerably in motivation from inter-school project work involving e-mail and text-based conferencing, the systems enabling teachers to provide them with higher-level work, thus preventing the onset of either boredom or attention-seeking behaviour (S2.2.63-64).

22. As these examples illustrate, one of the most striking gains for learners who have special needs has been in terms of motivation and self-confidence:

> Boys and girls of all ages, abilities and backgrounds are displaying equal and high levels of expertise with ICT, and willingly and confidently share and discuss their skills and knowledge with others, including their teachers. It is difficult to think of another area of school life, let alone the curriculum, where this occurs.
>
> (A3.67)

23. Serious problems of access could be experienced by children in small rural schools, where broadband networks (and therefore the ICT systems that require them) might not be provided. As one evaluation team point out:

> [For small rural schools] electronic communications... provide a form of enfranchisement for teachers and pupils, providing them with the kind of intellectual stimulus and social contact which those from larger schools take for granted... However, there is a danger that such potential will not be realised in rural schools, precisely because of their remote location. It is likely that the infrastructure will not be as highly developed in rural Scotland as, for example, in south east England, where the potential user base of services such as cable is many times greater, and some applications are restricted as a result.
>
> (S3.8-9)

24. Where the new technologies were successfully established and used in classrooms, they did begin to produce learning benefits, and to affect teacher-learner relationships in several important ways. However, there were significant differences in how each kind of system contributed to accessing and creating resources, and enabling learners to ommunicate electronically, so each of the three activities will be treated separately.

Accessing resources

25. Perhaps the simplest of the three activities is that in which the network is used to access electronic resources from beyond the classroom. Such resources were most commonly taken from the Internet, but a few projects experimented with accessing CD-ROMs held at a distant site, and one trialled an interactive TV system as part of a larger, non-educationally focused pilot scheme (D2.1.1).

26. Obtaining resources from Internet sites was one of the most popular activities within the Initiative, although there was concern that much of the language used in materials written largely for adults was too difficult for younger children.

27. Another anxiety was that learners would find undesirable material. Evaluation teams' findings varied on this point (B3.39, D3.43).

28. Teachers across the projects were well aware of this potential problem, and a variety of strategies were used to deal with it. Four broad approaches (A3.42-47) to controlling and monitoring learners' access to Internet resources can be identified:

- providing a 'walled garden' in which the Internet service provider selects what is included

- providing a filtered system which allows learners to access anything on the Internet that has not been filtered out because it has specific characteristics

- providing open access to the whole Internet but only under a degree of supervision by teachers, other adults or 'Internet prefects'

- setting up an honour system (sometimes combined with sanctions such as exclusion from the system) or alerting learners to the fact that teachers could trace which sites had been visited.

29. There is as yet no obvious way of establishing the relative merits or effects of these approaches. The Leicester team observed:

> While screening mechanisms of one kind or another were generally regarded as appropriate for younger learners, the tension between maintaining vigilance and encouraging students to develop responsible attitudes becomes more acute for teachers of older pupils. The solution preferred by a few schools was to provide open access, where pupils were allowed access to networks, but under close supervision. As systems become more accessible, however, complete control becomes more difficult. Those that favour these more open approaches, therefore, argue that it is preferable to teach responsibility, rather than operate a form of censorship. As one teacher put it, when discussing systems for controlling pupils' access, 'The most effective tool is education'.
>
> (A3.47)

30. Where CD-ROMs were tried out, two arrangements were used for extending access. One simple, yet successful, approach used in the Hertfordshire Link Centre project was to use surface mail to exchange single CDs on demand between co-operating training centres (B2.9.8). The other involved electronic transfer in which the discs were kept at a central location, with other sites then accessing the resources as required. This proved technically successful, as a way of making resources such as integrated learning systems (ILS) available (B3.41), although a 'jukebox' system planned for another project never became

operational (A2.1.14). Schools in the Kent Broadband Learning project used CD-ROM based resources extensively as a structured complement to Internet material (A2.3.70–71), while in the Superhighways in Education project (based in Essex and Kent) schools linked CD-ROM resources productively both with the Internet and with conventional library access (D2.3.40–41). This is one of the areas where questions of site licences and copyright protection will need to be given careful attention.

31. In the project trialling interactive TV (D2.1), material first needed to be reworked (digitised) for use on the system. Consequently, it was not possible to provide teachers with early access to a wide range of resources. At the end of the project, some primary schools felt there was little value in continuing to a wider trial without BBC and Channel 4 programmes being more widely available (D3.61).

32. An open integrated learning system (OILS) tried out in a few projects evoked mixed responses. Staff in one special school and in a special needs unit in another school (A2.1.77–79, A2.4.65) were highly enthusiastic. However, staff working with other students generally reacted less favourably (A2.1.83–84, A2.4.61, B2.3.75). One possibility is that the particular system used in the projects needed more preliminary investigation by teachers and more directed use in classrooms than it sometimes received (A2.4.65, A2.1.73). The Leicester team suggested that one productive strategy for achieving this was to arrange for older pupils to tutor younger ones (A3.70).

33. Working with the Internet encouraged a number of changes in the roles of teachers and learners. In particular, there was some evidence that it:

- made the teacher's role less instructional and more facilitative (A3.27)

- increased the proportion of independent 'home work' done by learners (D3.33)

- enabled learners to use a wider range of non-school resources for homework (D3.41)

- led some students to feel that they could organise their work better (D2.3.47)

- encouraged greater use of conventional information sources (D3.6)

- both required and encouraged learners to place more emphasis on creative thinking and problem solving (A3.28)

- increased differentiation (A3.28)

- promoted peer tutoring as a mutually beneficial activity (A3.7)

- encouraged some shift towards project work and an integrated curriculum (A3.41, D3.33).

34. The systems available for accessing resources offer different educational possibilities and are at different stages of development. The Internet is clearly already a viable classroom resource for general use, although at present the value for younger children may be somewhat restricted, and there is a definite need for teachers to set up clear, well-structured tasks if learners are not to get drawn into aimless browsing. The teaching of research and information-handling skills is also essential.

35. A huge and growing network of Internet sites already exists and, as a wide and diverse range of providers set up sites that draw together lists of useful resources on specific topics, it is becoming steadily easier to locate interesting resources. Indeed,

in many project schools and colleges, enthusiastic teachers have been establishing their own sites of this sort, or identifying existing sites and making them easily accessible to learners and other teachers. Outside these more ordered locations, the free electronic search engines available on the Internet give opportunities for more adventurous individualised study, so there is considerable scope for differentiation. Obtaining resources from the Internet does not involve other schools or colleges, so there is no need to co-ordinate timetables across institutions, and there is a relatively gentle cost gradient for schools and colleges wanting to start to develop their use of ICT with narrowband 'read-only' use of the Internet.

36. CD-ROMs too are already recognised as a viable classroom resource. The information on them is generally better structured than that available on the Internet, and they are in several respects more manageable both for learners and for teachers. If the provision of CD-ROM titles via networks is to be of value, however, it may require either large numbers of titles to be available at the central site, or the provision of a small set of CD-ROM titles of direct relevance to a closely defined teacher audience. As the Leeds team noted in their discussion of the GEMISIS 2000 Schools project, attention will need to be given to potential difficulties with copyright (B2.3.57–60) and technological problems (B2.3.66).

37. In the case of the interactive TV system that was trialled, the technology certainly has considerable possibilities, but it is at present best viewed as experimental. Until a substantial body of resources is made available in the new format and fully explored in a well planned and executed project, it will be

difficult to make a fair assessment of the educational merits of the system.

38. The OILS tried out in the Initiative is clearly capable of benefiting learners in some circumstances, and there is no doubt scope for further improvement. It is also clear that it is entirely practicable to deliver it over a multi-site network. Unlike some other integrated learning systems, it requires a significant input from teachers, and it is possible that the period of time it was in use in the EDSI schools was too short for the full benefits to emerge. However, the limited evidence from the EDSI projects suggests that it is not yet certain that OILS assists the full range of students for which it is intended. It is therefore perhaps best seen at this stage as useable in many situations but not yet a system that can be recommended for universal use.

Creating resources

39. As well as drawing upon external materials, many of the projects involved learners in creating various kinds of resources for use by themselves and others, for distribution either via the Internet or by more conventional means. Learners of all ages were able to take part in producing such materials. The Rosendale Odyssey project, for instance, was located in an infant school, where taking digital photographs was a feature of the work (A2.5.2). These were subsequently incorporated in the school's Internet pages.

40. As has already been noted, the creation of school and college Internet Web pages proved particularly popular, and some projects, such as the Highdown Information Hub, developed this activity much further (D2.2.40).

Creation of material of a complexity that specifically exploited the potential of broadband networks and applications was less common within the Initiative. However, the production of CD-ROMs (B2.5.20–21, B2.1.38–40) and the production or compilation of resources for display through an interactive TV system (D2.1) provide examples.

41. The creation of electronic resources is clearly a valuable ICT-based activity and an essential element in acquiring full network literacy. The use of a digital camera is well within the capabilities of most learners, and the technology is stable and now widely available. Many projects showed that young learners could develop the often complex skills needed to create material for individual Web pages, while the Acorn Home-School Links project successfully demonstrated that the creation of a substantial body of technologically sophisticated Web pages is also a viable option for older learners (in this case, sixth formers), given suitable teacher assistance (D2.1.44). As the London Colleges Multimedia Initiative has shown, there is clear evidence that the production of even more complex resources is within the reach of older students on specialist courses. This form of training would have considerable vocational relevance for many learners.

Electronic communication

42. Of the three learning activities, electronic communication involved the most diverse range of technologies. These fell into two groups. In one, the communication between sender and receiver is synchronous (in effect, instantaneous). Video conferencing has this characteristic. So too does text-based discussion, a variant on e-mail or text-based conferencing which requires instant response. This

is usually called a chat facility (as in, for instance, Internet Relay Chat, or distant chat), a label which perhaps underplays the educational potential it may have if systematically used. In most cases, though, the communication was asynchronous (that is, the message was stored in some way after arrival so that the recipient could retrieve and respond to it when convenient). E-mail, fax, and text-based conferencing have this characteristic. The distinction between synchronous and asynchronous systems had considerable importance in the classroom context.

43. **Fax machines**, although not included in the initial brief, proved surprisingly effective for both curriculum and management purposes. In one small rural primary school (S2.1.88), children and teachers were between them sending four faxes a day, a rate which the evaluation team thought typical. In the same project, a group of heads used both fax and e-mail to deal with routine inter-school matters prior to meeting over a video-conferencing link. As a result, it became possible for the number of such meetings to be reduced (S2.1.89), with significant savings in time and money.

44. **E-mail**, too, has been taken up in a large number of projects. In one school, children used it to contact parents living or working abroad (D3.55). One significant development has been the international school-to-school contacts it has made possible. In the Powys Access for Schools project, for example, one bilingual Welsh secondary school has begun to develop links with schools with shared linguistic interests, not only in Wales, but also in Eire, Germany, Denmark, Belgium and New Zealand – the last being a Maori school (A2.7.38).

45. In a similar way, a special school participating in the Furness Highway project used e-mail to establish links with other schools around the world. The use of a text-based asynchronous medium did not disadvantage learners who needed some time to compose their messages. The other schools were not told that the learners had any disabilities (B2.7.22–24).

46. With e-mail there is a potential issue of access by children to confidential communications sent or received by teachers. One solution to this was for teachers to have their own mailbox, with a shared facility for a class of pupils (A3.21). It should be noted that children need to be alerted to take care what personal details they include in messages, and advised on how to deal with unsolicited e-mails from someone they do not know.

47. **Text-based conferencing** has been a major feature in two projects for rural schools (S2.1.21, S2.2.14), where it has been part of an integrated approach which also used fax, e-mail and video conferencing. In one project it was used (alongside e-mail) to facilitate co-operative work by children across schools, with cross-school teams set up to work together on a shared curriculum project involving problem-solving and communication skills (S2.2.52–57). In some cases, text-based conferencing systems allow graphics and other kinds of files to be exchanged as well as text, but within the Initiative the focus appears to have been on the basic mode of use. However, the availability of file transfer facilities within several of the systems used for communications meant that the distinction between communicating and creating/accessing resources was somewhat blurred. (The STARS and Argyll and Bute projects, for

example, involved projects in which all three elements were involved.)

48. A few projects (S2.2.43, A2.2.59–60) tried out text-based discussion facilities, but these appear to have received only limited use. Some teachers were sceptical about the educational value, although the system appears to have been technically reliable. This medium may well have more educational potential than is immediately apparent but, if so, the Initiative does not indicate what this might be.

49. One issue that arises with e-mail, text-only conferencing and text-based discussion is the impact that these kinds of technologies will have upon the nature of English and Welsh as curriculum subjects. Providing, as they do, a hybrid means of communication that has some features of spoken communication and some features of written communication, these systems are creating entirely new writing genres, for which stylistic and social conventions are still evolving. Analogous issues will also arise with new multimedia forms, such as linked sets of Web pages and video conferencing, where equivalent changes in the nature of reading and writing are taking place. This will set teachers (and designers of national curricula) some particularly interesting challenges over the next few years.

50. **Video conferencing** was a feature of many projects. It was used not only for face-to-face discussion, but also for live video demonstrations, sharing computer applications, whiteboarding (the display and joint revision of pictures, plans and diagrams) and the transfer of files from one site to another. Of these applications, face-to-face discussion appears to be most commonly and confidently used,

although there are several examples of the others being successfully taken up.

51. A number of problems will need to be addressed before this medium is entirely suitable for general use in schools and colleges.

52. In the early stages of the Initiative, the systems were nearly all provided in what one might call 'telephone' mode, being set up to link individuals or small groups at two sites at any one time, although multi-site sessions were possible with at least one of the systems used. Another way of increasing the numbers of active participants in a two-site setting was to provide big screens for class viewing. The Live-Links project strategy for increasing levels of active participation was to combine a large viewing screen and a moderator who collected and passed on questions to the other site (E2.1.8). The question of group size is highly significant in terms of the cost effectiveness of these systems, as one-to-one teaching is obviously extremely expensive. If no way is found to support better teacher–learner ratios, there will be a tendency to restrict activities either to some form of peer tutoring exchange, or to situations such as careers interviews, where one-to-one meetings would be the norm anyway. Valuable as these approaches are, they do not make the most of the system's potential.

53. A second problem was that, while the various systems used were generally compatible when simple two-site discussions were involved, it was sometimes impossible to find ways of using other facilities (such as whiteboarding) across different systems (A2.4.12, B2.6.72). This lack of full compatibility severely restricts the educational potential of the medium.

show some of the ways in which the issues were tackled

- a consideration of the implications for future development.

Training issues

131. Within the projects, training was given by one or more providers of various kinds, including:

    - the companies involved (D2.3.20, B2.3.45, A2.5.13)

    - education authority based groups (C2.1.4, C2.2.1, S1.1.32–34)

    - outside organisations (A2.3.28)

    - academics from the project team (A2.5.14, S2.2.26)

    - staff colleagues (A2.3.31)

    - pupils (A2.3.28, A2.1.32).

132. The groups receiving training included IT technicians (B2.5.60) and parents (D2.2.21–23), but in this part of the report, as in the EDSI projects overall, the focus will be largely on provision for teachers.

133. Teachers were usually given technical training in using ICT systems, and sometimes help in identifying and trying out promising educational uses for them. In some projects there was confusion over the division of responsibility for meeting these two requirements. Some companies assumed (incorrectly) that, if they provided technical training, the educational possibilities would immediately be apparent (B3.24, A3.8, C2.2.4–7). In other cases, little or no technical training was provided (A2.4.27, D2.1.31) and, in a number of projects, schools felt they needed more support than they received.

134. The amount of formal training provided varied widely from project to project. In one project where students and staff from all participating secondary

schools were given the option of taking a telematics certificate, around 60 students took this up (B2.4.19).

135. Formal and informal face-to-face training was supplemented in various ways. These included running helplines (A2.6.36), an illustrated user guide (B2.4.48), training materials devised by teachers for other teachers (S2.1.33), the use of commercial training videos (D2.2.18), and staff learning by doing (with varying degrees of support from colleagues) through producing CD-ROMs for student use (B2.5.26–32). Providing a variety of types of learning opportunities within a programme was seen as important (D3.20).

136. Placing training appropriately within the project schedule was important, but delays in installation often caused difficulties. In one case (A2.2.18), this led to training sessions being held before the teachers had received the equipment, which meant they could not follow up the experience. In another case, the consultants – whose main remit had been to develop the educational potential of the software supplied – were largely diverted into providing training on equipment which arrived late (A2.1.25–26).

137. Where training time was very limited, the question of breadth versus depth in training became important, particularly in those projects where two or more quite different kinds of ICT were being introduced together. In the light of their EDSI observations, the Leicester team concluded that, where possible, initial training should be given in one system or application at a time (A3.86).

138. The potential of the new technologies themselves for training is a key issue for any future national development, and much of what was said earlier in

this report about the different systems is relevant here. The Internet, interactive TV and CD-ROM (not to mention print and conventional TV) all offer ways of conveying bodies of factual material, while video conferencing and text-based conferencing offer media through which staff can obtain help in interpreting and applying this material from expert tutors, and from formal and informal self-help networks. The Lingu@NET project offered an example of Internet-based professional development, while the CLASS project showed CD-ROM and video conferencing being used for professional development.

139. In addition, several teams (A2.6.23, B2.4.51, C2.1, C2.2) reported projects using, or planning to use, video conferencing for IT training or support. In at least two projects (the Dyfed Satellite project and the BEON project), some training in the use of video conferencing was conducted by distant trainers via the medium itself (A2.6.19–21, A2.1.29).

Five approaches to training the teachers

140. A comparison of training provision in five representative projects shows how certain teams approached these matters, and with what results. The five projects are:

    - Teachers Managing Learning (TML)

    - Bristol Education On-Line Network (BEON)

    - Modern Communications for Teaching and Learning in Argyll and Bute

    - CLASS project

    - Multimedia Portables for Teachers Pilot.

141. These projects differed in their degree of formality and in the extent to which training in the use of ICT was

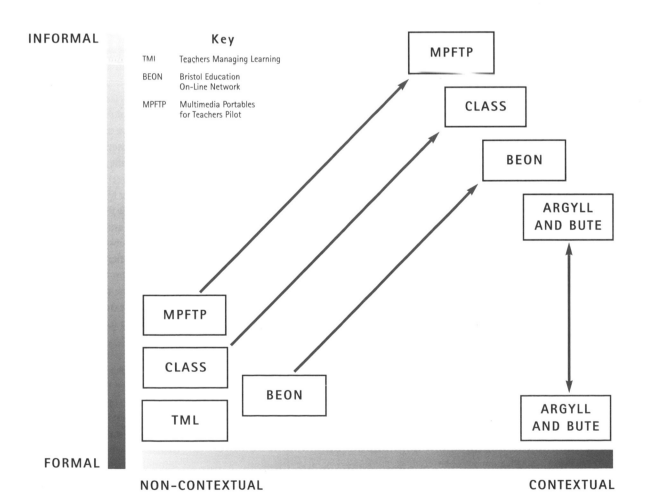

adjusted to suit the specific educational context in which a recipient worked (see Diagram 1). The former influenced who might be a potential trainer, the degree of constraint over location and scheduling of training and whether formal assessment and certification were appropriate. The degree of contextualisation of training for individual recipients influenced many of these features, but also affected the potential cost per person and the means by which information was presented and/or explored by them too.

142. The Teachers Managing Learning project (C2.2) was centrally prepared by a group of LEA agencies and started with a no-charge programme of ICT awareness-raising sessions. These were face-to-face sessions in local centres, made available to all schools in the authority, in which the Internet and video conferencing were demonstrated and tried out. The team then invited schools to opt in to a second phase of development where they would buy in assistance from authority support staff for an ICT development project of their choice. The TML Phase 1 training was not linked to any specific development in the schools, thus exemplifying a formal and non-contextual approach.

143. The philosophy of open access here contrasted strongly with the more selective approach of most projects, and thus provided some evaluation data on a substantial number of schools that were not pre-selected. In this respect, the experiences of this project team provide a far better sense of the problems of national dissemination than any of the others.

144. The first phase was well received by the participants but only 12 schools out of 170 Phase 1 participants expressed any sustained interest in the second phase. This may have been because of the difficulty of building in at short notice additional costs to their five-year plans.

INFORMAL

Key

TMI	Teachers Managing Learning
BEON	Bristol Education On-Line Network
MPFTP	Multimedia Portables for Teachers Pilot

FORMAL

NON-CONTEXTUAL   **CONTEXTUAL**

Diagram 1 Patterns of staff development in five EDSI projects – arrows indicate the direction of changes in programmes over time

162. In a similar way, the position of initial trainers will need review, as will the national requirements for initial teacher education; given the lead times involved, this demand may be quite urgent. Less obviously, adjustment may be needed to several other professional development initiatives, such as the training for head teachers, some education authority staff and any qualification intended to recognise expert teachers. The dissemination of ICT-based changes into schools and colleges will place quite new management demands upon heads and principals. The role of IT co-ordination, too, will change radically once IT has become ICT. The Lancaster team note that:

> The role and responsibilities of the co-ordinator will be vital to the development of ICT practice within schools. In terms of the professional development needs for co-ordinators, key issues are:
>
> - understanding the role and responsibilities involved
>
> - knowing about a range of possible uses of ICT resources
>
> - appropriate deployment and location of equipment
>
> - the means to develop resources
>
> - being able to develop teams to create Web pages and materials
>
> - identifying appropriately when, where and how IT and information skills are taught (whether it be in PSE, core lessons, cross-curricular, or outside main school lesson times).
>
> (D.3.25)

163. This assumes that the scope, as distinct from the range, of these posts will remain essentially the same as for many IT co-ordinators now. However, it may be that a quite different kind of post will be needed. Establishing, managing and exploiting an evolving network of external relationships with business people, with senior staff in local schools and colleges, and with schools across the world will be very different from managing face-to-face relationships within a familiar institution. Whether these aspects of the work are carried by a redefined ICT co-ordinator post or taken up by another member of staff will no doubt vary from situation to situation: the key point is that these new tasks will need to be covered systematically in some way.

Building a learning community: supporting learning at local, regional and national level

164. The notion of a learning institution emphasises the need to change internal relationships and processes, but this only partly addresses the challenges presented by technologies that create a network of links between people and resources that reaches far beyond an individual school or college. The notion of the learning community complements this by directing attention towards the ways in which schools or colleges establish links both to other educational institutions and to the local community.

165. As the Lancaster team point out, each of the EDSI projects had to create and develop a related set of physical, resource and human networks (D3.101). Using this classification, the role of ICT in building a learning community can be explored by looking in sequence at:

- how projects differed in the physical, resource and human networks they developed, and the advantages of each approach

- how projects handled the start-up phase

- how the projects subsequently developed, and why

- the implications for the national development of learning communities.

How projects differed in physical, resource and human networks

166. Two issues arise concerning the physical networks: the bandwidth required, and the relative merits of different means of transmission (such as cable or telephone line) to be used.

167. Some Internet material was obtained over narrowband networks, but there were nearly always gains in efficiency and speed if intermediate or broadband networks were employed instead. The evaluation teams did not entirely dismiss narrowband for downloading Internet resources, but there was general agreement that it was tedious to use. In addition, broadband and intermediate systems offered ways of obtaining resources not realistically available over narrowband systems. Examples within the Initiative included:

- databases of material obtained ultimately from remote sensing satellite monitoring (A2.6)

- TV programmes stored on a central project server (D2.1)

- real-time transmissions from remote video cameras (C2.2.19–20, E2.1.6–10)

- CD-ROMs held elsewhere (D2.3.16–19, B2.3).

168. If all learners are to have ready access to ICT, then a universally accessible infrastructure of networks will be needed, initially providing intermediate bandwidth access, but moving as quickly as possible to broadband level.

169. In addition to bandwidth variations, the kinds of transmission networks

used each had other distinctive advantages and disadvantages for educational use. This was considered in some depth by the Lancaster team, who distinguished four forms of communication technologies giving access to resources and other users, namely:

- conventional telephone and ISDN (Integrated Services Digital Network) links

- cable TV infrastructure

- ATM (asynchronous transfer mode) networks

- radio communication.

170. The team observed that:

Within this evaluation, performance of both cable-network access and iTV access through an ATM system have not led to any identifiable problems which sponsors have not been able or willing to solve. Where problems have occurred, these have been concerned more with delays in connectivity, rather than with performance of systems once connections have been completed. The speed that cable systems have offered has not, of course, solved the problems of delays at certain times of day when the number of connections to remote servers is high. During the afternoon, for example, access to the Internet can be as slow through a cable link as through a telephone link.

Particular features of each linking technology offer certain advantages. For example, cable modems provide greater speeds of delivery than traditional modems. The ATM system used has demonstrated certain advantages that this networking technology can offer – for example:

- reliable transfer of multimedia, video, audio, and graphical data

- ability to transfer synchronised video with other data forms

- rapid connection to a variety of information sources.

Schools need to be aware fully of the advantages and disadvantages of each linking technology, and the range of future implications, if they are also to understand commercial pressures in this area.

(D3.46–47)

171. The team went on to draw attention to several technological points that arose from the evaluation and which they considered required particular attention in the future. They noted that:

- future inter-operability may well be dependent upon developments of agreements on standards in a range of areas

- schools could become 'locked in' to proprietary, non-standard systems

- considerations need to be made with regard to security of material accessible, both that authored by the schools, and that being accessed

- the encoding and storage services for multimedia provision may require particular conditions and levels of investment, such as more expensive computers

- it cannot be assumed that future access to material will be automatic or free

- expertise in courseware production is limited currently to particular skills and interests developed by certain individuals.

Schools will need to consider whether commercial providers offering networking provision are likely to tie them into particular hardware and software which will not provide a desirable or necessary openness and inter-operability. [...] While most organisations and companies recognise the need for open solutions, when standards are not yet finalised or do not exist there is the possibility that some providers may develop a 'unique' solution. [...]

Issues of inter-operability between what are currently resource and physical intranets need to be considered as a matter of urgency. There should be a focus upon project developments which enable this issue to be examined. Some industrial project personnel are convinced currently that adherence to Internet standards will be sufficient; this case does not appear, however, for schools accessing systems, to have been fully tested through this evaluation.

(D3.48–50)

172. The networks of educational resources potentially available to projects fell into three main kinds: namely, Web resources, digitised video/TV and CD-ROM. These were discussed earlier in this report.

173. However, the projects involved more than computers, physical networks and resources; they also depended upon the creation of human networks. These took a number of different forms in the EDSI projects (see Table 6), but with a strong bias towards projects built around locally based groups. These different patterns offer different possibilities to participants (see Table 7).

174. Single-age-range clusters (such as those comprising only local primary schools) allow for joint curriculum and staff development and the exchange of resource materials and ideas. On the other hand, co-operation in such clusters might be hampered if the participants were competing with each other for learners.

175. Where schools or colleges are in active competition, other patterns of linkage may fit their requirements better. One structure that emerged in some projects (although not necessarily because those involved favoured a competitive strategy) was that of a single institution linked to several current or potential feeder

service that provides and maintains the physical network only, and one that includes curriculum resource provision as an integral part of the package. The danger with the latter arrangement is that teachers might find that they were locked into an arrangement that did not allow them sufficient professional control over curriculum content. This is not, of course, to say that the purchasing of commercial software and resources is undesirable, but only that if schools and colleges are to retain maximum freedom over which of these resources they take up, they need to ensure that future decisions are not foreclosed by the nature of the arrangements agreed for providing and supporting the physical network.

187. Faced with a novel situation and very little shared experience to go on, the project teams initially had difficulties in identifying the right training provision although, as indicated above, nearly all projects eventually felt their way through to a workable approach.

188. Once the physical network was in place, resource networks were accessed with varying degrees of ease. In some cases, the creation of resources by learners and by staff in the school or college also went well, although the emphasis in several projects shifted towards using rather than creating – often in response to difficulties encountered when attempting the latter.

189. Overall, the picture that emerged from the start-up phase is of great enthusiasm, considerable (but diverse and sometimes unco-ordinated) relevant skills and knowledge, variable quality in project management, slow physical installation and some initial delays in identifying and setting up viable forms of training. In total, the effect

of this was to extend the setting-up phase in nearly all the projects beyond what everyone had anticipated. This in turn significantly reduced the time available for the projects and the evaluation teams to gain a clear picture of how the various systems were best used in classrooms and other learning locations.

How the projects evolved

190. How the projects evolved once the basic infrastructure and training was complete varied from case to case. One important influence was whether the initial thrust for the project came from the educational side or the technical side. The Leicester team noted (A3.8–11) that technology-led approaches left schools uncertain about the educational purposes to which the technology should be put. Consequently, reluctant to abandon unsuitable systems in case it offended the sponsors, they tended to take on applications because they felt they should. This points to the need for some kind of 'honest broker' with expertise in educational applications and a sound knowledge of the culture of schools.

191. The FE colleges involved appear to have been relatively autonomous from the outset in their relationships with companies. Schools often started out more dependent than colleges upon the companies they worked with but, as the projects developed, showed movement to a far more assertive stance:

> During the lifetime of these projects, power relationships have tended to change. At first, schools were anxious to comply with their sponsors' wishes, even when they thought they were educationally unsound, lest the support they were receiving should be taken away. However, by the time the projects were due to end, schools had

begun to realise that they were in a stronger position since, if partnership ended in acrimony, sponsors would have no examples of good practice to show prospective clients when endeavouring to promote their services. In this way, both sides have come to realise that they need each other and a more co-operative responsive partnership has developed which augurs well for the future.

(A3.85)

192. At first, the relationship between companies and schools was one where the nature of the benefits to both was unclear. As a more accurate picture emerged, expectations and attitudes changed. The risk was that, if both sides' initial expectations were not met, disillusionment and subsequent withdrawal of active involvement could result (D3.97–100).

193. In such cases, before a joint project is taken on there is a need to establish clearly what the ground rules for co-operation will be. One of the benefits from EDSI is that there is now some experience of such joint ventures to draw upon for the future.

194. Relationships between the various schools and colleges within a project showed changes – in this case from isolation to varying degrees of co-operation, and from initial equality of aspiration to eventual inequality of achievement.

195. Often schools and colleges began by aiming to get their own houses in order before turning outwards to other project schools and colleges. Developing effective human networking between the project institutions was almost invariably difficult and, in some cases, not achieved in any substantial way (A2.7.34–40, D2.1.48, D2.3.34). More typically, some of the schools or

colleges in a project (but not all) established strong links with each other – as, for example, in the Kent Broadband Learning project and the Knowledge Superhighways project in Birmingham (A2.4.20, A2.3.100). In only one case did a strong and fully inclusive network emerge (S2.1.41–49). It is probably significant that this particular project evolved out of a professional community in which co-operation was already an established value. The project also displayed a mix of individual school initiatives, local subgroupings and strong, yet responsive, central management. These features were all present before the electronic network was introduced, and the project itself was explicitly designed to strengthen those arrangements.

196. It should be noted that some projects were set up in ways that envisaged fairly restricted linkages from the outset. This might take the form of a project having a set of largely separate subgroups, with interaction taking place within the

subgroups (B2.5.1) or, alternatively, a single institution acting as a nodal point, with most communication being between that member and the others individually (F2.2, B2.2, F2.3).

197. One inevitable result of these differences in activity was that what individual schools and colleges got from their projects varied, even if they had all intended originally to gain equally from their involvement (A2.4.19–26). At this stage it is impossible to say whether this is an intrinsic feature of such networks, or simply an indication that the EDSI project groups have not yet been going long enough to develop a strong identity and sense of shared purpose.

Implications for future development

198. One clear message from the evaluation (A3.12, D3.114–117) is that the starting point for planning a learning community should be to agree jointly the needs of the groups

involved; decisions about the physical network and resources required follow from that. However, it is clear from the most successful EDSI projects that, once these networks are in place and begin to be used, the experience feeds back into the thinking of the participants at every level, creating a dynamic and evolving pattern of development (see Diagram 2). The strong impression from the projects is that an electronically-based learning community will only maintain the involvement of new ICT users if it largely maps on to their existing personal or professional connections, at least to begin with. Furthermore, those involved must have some sense of shared identity, or a realistic expectation that each participant has both something to gain from, and something to give to, other members.

199. The specific implications of this for schools and FE colleges are distinctly different, so they will be considered separately.

200. For schools, a clear need emerges (see Diagram 3) for three kinds of support:

- a strong web of local connections

- a much looser and more intermittent set of links to a wide variety of national and international organisations, individuals and resources

- a local, regional and national support infrastructure to encourage and sustain these various networks.

Diagram 3 summarises the kind of network of contacts and access to resources that this implies for an individual school.

201. To meet the first requirement, a roughly 'project-sized' cluster of neighbouring schools would be

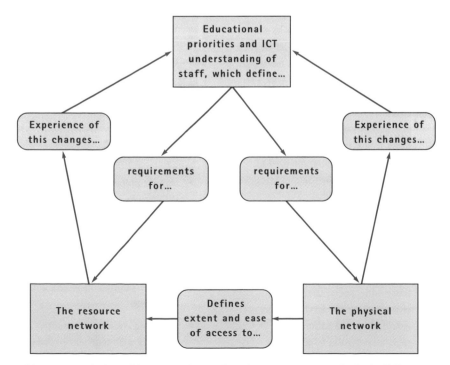

Diagram 2 Roles of human, physical and resource networks in building a learning community

improvement both in ICT and also in the capacity of all schools and colleges to make good use of it?

216. It is now clear that the answers to these three questions are to some degree interdependent. Very well managed and experienced schools and colleges can make something of underdeveloped or unreliable technologies, even without much project support. Fairly poorly placed schools can promote learning with good technologies and timely and appropriate support through the project infrastructure, but similar schools may well fail to do so under less promising conditions. Middling schools can, given strong project support, make a great deal of middling technologies.

217. To maximise opportunities for learning, improvements will be needed in present institutions, technologies and infrastructure. A crucial requirement will be to ensure that, while progress is made as rapidly as possible, no school or college is encouraged to try more than it can realistically manage. What is needed is both to create the scaffolding for a learning society by providing ICT-ready schools and colleges with the established ICT technologies, while at the same time developing both the remaining schools and colleges and the remaining technologies to draw them into this evolving network.

Evaluating the readiness of the technologies

218. In the educational context, any ICT technology intended for universal take-up needs to be:

- demonstrably educationally valuable
- widely available
- affordable
- reliable

- technically supportable
- useable by any appropriate teacher and any appropriate learner.

219. In these terms, technologies investigated in the EDSI projects can be provisionally classified as follows.

a) Established technologies that meet all these criteria in full:

- fax
- e-mail
- text-based conferencing
- Internet sites used by learners for accessing resources
- CD-ROMs.

b) Useable technologies that meet all these criteria to a minimum level and some of the criteria (which must include educational value) in full:

- Internet pages and sites produced by learners
- the open integrated learning system that was used
- video conferencing.

220. Experimental technologies that fail to meet some criteria at even a minimal level, but which show sufficient educational and commercial potential to be worth further investigation are:

- text-based discussion
- interactive TV.

221. The classification of technologies will change as costs reduce, and as technical capabilities and the capacity of teachers and learners to use different kinds of equipment and resources improve. Furthermore, the flow of innovations shows no signs of abating. The emergence, for example, of Internet sites which push resources out automatically to subscribers is a development that has significant educational

implications. What is needed is not a single set of decisions now about what to do about ICT, but arrangements that ensure that technological developments are routinely encouraged, trialled, evaluated and systematically considered for universal adoption for educational use as they reach an acceptable level of development.

Evaluating the readiness of schools and colleges

222. The introduction of ICT to all schools and colleges will clearly require a phased programme of development. The experience from the Initiative suggests that the best strategy for this would be to build local and national networks, starting with what might be called the ICT-ready schools and colleges. These would be ones which already have:

- staff and governors wishing to introduce or expand ICT provision
- suitable arrangements and staffing in place or planned for managing the innovation
- a basic core of staff with prior experience of IT use, and generally positive attitudes towards it.

Possible markers for the last two criteria are given in paragraphs 102 and 104 above.

223. The first task in such a development programme would be to identify formally these ICT-ready institutions, and to ensure that they received the necessary funding, training and external support to enable them to introduce or expand access to established forms of ICT. This first phase of development (together with the infrastructure provision discussed below) would provide the local and national networks needed to support the subsequent growth in the number of institutions involved.

224. The availability of already functioning local and national networks would effectively lower the management demands and levels of IT experience and enthusiasm required to allow other schools and colleges to join. The availability locally of 'first-phase' institutions would also allow staff and governors from other schools and colleges to see for themselves what was involved, and to obtain advice and support in preparing their own schools and colleges to join. This combination of a fully operational network and local sources of support and advice would create the conditions for an extended second phase of development, in which most other schools and colleges would progressively join the network as they became willing and able to do so.

225. It is possible that there would still remain a small number of institutions unable to become ICT-ready without substantial extra support; if so, such support would need to come under some wider, not ICT-related, programme for school and college improvement.

Developing the infrastructure

226. Given that the level of success achieved by project schools and colleges was in part a function of the support and resources that the project teams provided, an equivalent local infrastructure would be required. However, a regional and national infrastructure would be necessary, too.

227. Within the local infrastructure, mechanisms would be needed to:

- organise the grouping of all schools into neighbourhood clusters, each with a cluster co-ordinator, technical support, a cluster budget and a fully compatible and easily extended network linking the participants

- provide support at education authority level for the cluster co-ordinators through the internal or external provision of advice and training on management and curriculum issues

- encourage and support links between the schools and other local partners such as parents, business, libraries and colleges

- arrange the provision (either at cluster or education authority level) of a managed service for the physical network

- ensure local availability of key categories of staff, such as ICT-competent IT co-ordinators and ICT-competent advisers

- assist ICT companies in identifying suitable schools and colleges for the further trialling and improvement of experimental and useable, but not yet established, technologies.

228. Nationally and regionally, mechanisms would be needed to:

- identify ICT-ready schools

- agree an overall policy for linking funding from different sources to the ICT development programme, and to provide a mechanism for implementing this policy

- set up a coherent set of national Internet sites to support different groups of teachers and other staff, each site to provide a one-stop shop for obtaining information and contacts to assist with professional and curriculum development issues

- ensure that relevant changes were made to national curricula, initial teacher training and continuing professional development as required

- systematically review each useable technology with a view to its being upgraded to the status of an established technology

- systematically monitor developments in experimental technologies world-wide to assess their educational potential, with a view to developing suitable technologies into useable forms in the UK.

229. As each technology reached a point where it could be given established status this would (subject to funding being available) trigger the move to national dissemination and support. This would involve:

- making the technologies (including any necessary physical networking) available to all schools and colleges that were demonstrably ready and willing to take them

- simultaneous provision of targeted INSET support for staff (including relevant senior managers) in those schools and colleges

- inclusion of the use of that technology in relevant forms of continuing professional development and in initial teacher training, and a review of any implications for the various national curricula.

230. Questions of how present organisations and procedures would need to be adjusted to create this sort of infrastructure and programme go beyond the scope of this report, but some comment on resources is appropriate.

231. A central problem is how to provide secure long-term resources to develop the programme. This is in part a matter of funding, but not exclusively so. It is already clear that the introduction of ICT can be used by schools and colleges as a way of generating additional resources of

many kinds from the local community and beyond. All of these (except arguably those activities which simply shift 5–16 learners from one school to another) provide indirect benefits for current or future learners, and represent a very important means of encouraging institutional growth and community development.

232. Unfortunately, opportunities for different schools and colleges to gain access to several of these kinds of resource are often unequal. In general, smaller schools catering for younger learners – especially in poorer or more sparsely populated areas – are probably going to attract less private (and public) funding per learner than others.

233. There is a risk that the popularity of ICT will draw learners and private sector resources disproportionately towards those schools that are already best placed to fund and further develop their existing ICT provision. If this in turn seriously de-stabilises other schools nearby, the resources that should have gone into developing the ICT capabilities of those schools may instead be diverted into providing stop-gap and emergency support at a far more basic level.

234. While more could be done to encourage schools and colleges to increase the proportion of internal funding they allocate to ICT, this alone is unlikely to be enough to cover the introduction of ICT. Nor will the additional resources created by involving parents and local companies, or by attracting more people back into education, cover the introduction of networks and systems into schools and colleges that do not yet have them. Such developments pre-suppose the availability of equipment and trained, enthusiastic staff: they do

not precede it. The benefits of ICT can feed the further growth of schools and colleges once they are started on the development process, but they are not themselves a starting point.

235. EDSI has had considerable success drawing in the ICT companies to act as funders and providers of support, but only a relatively small percentage of schools and colleges participated in the Initiative. It is hard to see how the ICT industry could assume responsibility for funding the remainder at the same level, although it certainly has a continuing contribution to make in research and product development and by setting education prices and tariffs at reasonable levels.

236. It is clear that schools will need assistance if they are to become well-informed customers for ICT systems and support. The Departments have therefore funded NCET to produce a good-practice and decision-making guide to the education superhighway, drawing on the EDSI evaluations and other sources, to assist schools with this task. It will be important for schools and colleges to review the priority they are giving to new technologies in terms of resourcing, and for there to be sufficient seedcorn funding available from Government to help set these developments in motion within each school and college.

Meeting the challenge

237. Looking across the EDSI projects, one emerging pattern is clear. The introduction of ICT overcomes or blurs many different boundaries. These include the boundaries between subjects, between the academic and the social aspects of a topic or problem, between learners of different ages and abilities, between different categories of

teachers, between teachers and other adults as co-workers in supporting learners, between home and school, school and work, and between schools and colleges. These technologies have the capacity to dissolve some of the distinctions between the local neighbourhood and places far away, and between face-to-face and distance communication.

238. Very few of these effects are entirely new, but what is new is that the same set of technologies can produce them all, and in a stronger and increasingly more convergent form than previously. Furthermore, the technological complexities of ICT systems are substantial and the managerial and organisational demands made on all those introducing them will be considerable.

239. This will make for an extremely challenging national development programme, but the new technologies provide exciting opportunities for all those willing to help to create a learning society open to all. Whether all those involved are prepared to make the commitments needed to take up the challenge is now the central issue.

---

1   Schools considering entering into lease agreements must first ensure that any arrangements conform with the law and, in the case of LEA-maintained schools, are in accordance with the LEA's local management of schools (LMS) scheme.

References

Note:

This synoptic report draws from the full reports of the teams who evaluated the original EDSI projects. Where the main text refers to the source of the point being made in the relevant evaluation report, the references give – in order – group letter, section, project report (where applicable) and paragraph numbers. For how to find the full reports on the World Wide Web, see next page.

NCET, Group F – *Lingu@NET – A Virtual Language Centre: Interim Report,* NCET (May 1997)

Galton M., Comber C., Hargreaves L., Lawson T., Fogelman K., Thorpe R. and Roberts-Young D., *Group A – Curriculum Projects in England and Wales: Final Report,* University of Leicester School of Education in association with the University College of Wales, Aberystwyth (1997)

Grant J., Chambers E. and Mason R., *Group E – Higher and Professional Education: Final Report,* Joint Centre for Education in Medicine and Open University Institute of Educational Technology (1997)

Hall J., McPake J. and Somekh B., *Group S – Curriculum Projects in Scotland: Final Report,* Scottish Council for Research in Education (1997)

Harrison C., Youngman M., Bailey M., Fisher T., Phillips R. and Restorick J., *Group F – DfEE Multimedia Portables for Teachers Pilot: Evaluation Report,* University of Nottingham (Interim Report July 1997)

Higham J., Byard M., Engineer P., Hartley R., Horbury P., Jenkins I. and White D., *Group B – Vocationally-Focused Projects: Final Report,* Computer Based Learning Unit, School of Education, University of Leeds (1997)

McFarlane A., North R. and Strain M., *Group C – Teachers' Professional Development: Final Report,* Homerton College, Cambridge, and Magee College, University of Ulster (1997)

Passey D., Forsyth K., Hutchinson D., Scott A. and Williams N., *Group D – Home-School Links: Final Report,* Lancaster University (1997)

Selinger M., Taylor J., Kirkwood A., Littleton K., Wearmouth J., Lincoln C., Meadows J. and Davis P., *Group F – Educational Internet Service Providers Project Evaluation Study: Interim Report,* University of Warwick (March 1997)

Full Project Reports:
Finding them on the Web

The full text of these reports can be found on the Web at the following address: http://www.ncet.org.uk/edsi

When you reach the Web address, you can go directly to the report of your choice by entering its index number (see below) in the boxes you will see on the opening screen.

For example, if you want to look at the Group A report on the Kent Broadband Learning project, key A2 in the first box, 3 in the second box and – if you know which paragraph you want – put that number in the third box. If you are looking for the whole report rather than a specific paragraph, leave the third box blank.

To find a paragraph in either an executive summary or a cross-project report, enter the index number in the first box and the paragraph number in the third box, leaving the middle box blank. There is no need to key in the full points between the letters and numbers: simply enter the code letters and numbers in the boxes.

Appendices

EXECUTIVE SUMMARIES OF PROJECT REPORTS

Group A
Curriculum Projects in England and Wales
Executive Summary

The Projects

1. This evaluation concerns seven curriculum-focused projects that were based mainly in the primary and secondary sectors in England and Wales. Two further projects in the group were located in Scotland and were the subject of a separate report produced by the Scottish Council for Research in Education (SCRE) – see Appendix 2. The projects were extremely diverse in scale, ranging from a single infants school with two machines to a group of around 30 secondary schools and sixth form colleges exploring a range of technology. Projects also varied greatly in their organisational and technological structure, and in their aims and objectives. What united the group was a classroom focus, with teachers and pupils exploring the potential of a range of information and communications technology (ICT) to enhance teaching and learning.

Project A2.1: Bristol Education On-Line Project (BEON)

Description of the project

2. The project involved a group of primary schools, one secondary school and one special school, and was a trial of a managed network that enabled schools to have remote access to on-line interactive education services and applications, a 'walled garden' Internet environment and point-to-point video conferencing.

3. The special and primary schools each received 30 networked workstations; the secondary school received 200, as well as various peripherals such as colour printers. A PC in each school, three in the secondary school, were enhanced for desktop video conferencing. These were connected on a local area network (LAN), linked via BT ISDN2 lines to three remote servers which provided network management, access to the Internet and video conferencing. Schools also had remote access to an open integrated learning system (OILS) for English, mathematics and modern languages, a variety of standard applications, clip-art files and multimedia objects. For technical reasons, an original proposal for remote access to a CD-ROM library was never operational.

4. The main commercial sponsors in the project were BT and International Computers Ltd (ICL). ICL installed the school networks, while BT was responsible for the wide area components that position BEON as a true information superhighway project. BT installed high-bandwidth connections to the servers, ISDN lines for the video conferencing, and 2-megabit bearers to provide access to the network services such as CampusWorld, the Internet and e-mail. ICL provided remote on-line service management and also provided the CD-ROMs and local applications such as the integrated learning system (ILS). ICL undertook the initial training and also commissioned a team from the Education Department at Exeter University to provide remote and on-site INSET.

Aims and outcomes

5. The aims of the project were to explore the value, for both educational development of pupils and the professional development of teachers, of the curriculum materials and support services provided, and to weigh any added value in educational/professional terms against the real costs of such a service at full commercial rates. The measure of added value in educational terms focused mainly on the degree to which the technology enhanced the learning of the pupils, but consideration was also given to improvements in individual and social areas such as self-confidence and communication.

6. The project had a major impact on the culture of the schools and the motivation and confidence of children. Some schools reported gains in literacy, oracy and communication skills, as well as improved social skills. The proportion of pupils with special educational needs (SEN) in the schools was well above the national average and although, with the exception of the special school, little targeted project-related work was conducted with these pupils, the majority clearly benefited.

7. In general, pupils made intelligent use of Internet materials, and became adept at moving and manipulating information between different applications. There were, however, criticisms from teachers about the operation and content of the 'walled garden' World Wide Web (WWW) environment. OILS formed a major feature of their project activity in the secondary school. While, overall, the software failed to have the impact upon learning that was anticipated, schools were looking at ways in which to improve the technology and to identify optimum conditions for its use.

8. The role of the remote helpdesk, which provided rapid and reliable on-line technical support, was highly commended by the schools and was a central feature of the managed service. Much praise was also given to the Exeter University team who provided remote and on-site INSET for both teachers and pupils in particular applications, and one-to-one tuition with curriculum experts. Inter-school collaboration developed during the project, although, for a number of reasons, this diminished towards the end of the trial.

9. The special school for pupils with emotional and behavioural difficulties (EBD) was, in more ways than one, relatively isolated from the other schools in the project. The pupils came from extremely deprived social and economic backgrounds, and generally expressed very low levels of self-esteem, short attention spans and poor reading and writing ability. Nevertheless, the technology had a major impact in the school, and proved to be a highly motivating facility, was in constant use, and considerably increased the confidence of these pupils.

10. A variety of different 'visions' of the future are being discussed by teachers and managers, who are in the main hopeful of being able to build on the lessons learned so far. One area where there was unanimity was the desire for the schools to continue with a managed service, but to have greater 'ownership' over the project's direction.

11. The project had a considerable effect on the culture of the schools. The majority of both pupils and teachers became highly computer- and network-literate, and for pupils these gains were made regardless of age or ability. Most schools were, at the end of the trial, exploring ways of incorporating the technologies into schemes of work across the curriculum.

12. In a project of this scale and complexity, there were inevitably some difficulties, and these included management and technical issues as well as differences in the ways in which the different technologies were introduced and used in the classroom. In general, however, the project succeeded in enhancing teaching and learning through the use of ICT. Although it is difficult to quantify achievement gains in the relatively short time-scale of the trial, the majority of the staff and pupils had moved from novice status to expert in their understanding, competence and sophistication in the use of ICT; in particular, there were clear gains in self-esteem, motivation, confidence, and IT and networking skills. The commitment of the sponsors, school managers, teachers and particularly project co-ordinators was a key factor in bringing this about.

13. The model of a managed service was particularly effective, eventually allowing teachers to concentrate on curriculum, rather than technical, concerns. Teachers also praised the role of the team from Exeter University, who provided expertise and support for schools to develop purposeful curriculum-focused activities. Although the project represented a potentially costly model of delivering ICT, the combination of the managed approach, a broad range of networked services and the availability of curriculum support and development provided schools with highly valuable experience and a model of practice on which to build.

Costs and cost benefits

14. Despite some residual tension between the educational and commercial partners, the project achieved much, and demonstrated the viability of a managed service. However, at the end of the trial, it became clear that the true costs of a project of this scale and complexity were beyond the budgets of the schools. While the managed service was positively received by the schools, they were actively seeking alternative, lower-cost solutions towards the end of the project. However, last-minute negotiations resulted in a new phase, whereby the schools agreed to continue to act as a 'test-bed' in return for an extension to the trial.

Project A2.2: Project ConnectEd (also known as Project IntraNet)

Description of the project

15. ConnectEd involved three commercial organisations, 20 schools and colleges, and Guildford College. The initial aims of the project emphasised the exploration of the educational benefits of the Internet; the development of curriculum support materials and their availability via a network; sharing of resources via a network; encouraging the use of IT by teachers, pupils and parents; and the development of presentation skills. Thus the main project activities were to be the use of a dedicated Web site; the use of e-mail and video conferencing as means of communication between participants and others; and the use of the Internet as a source of information for students.

16. Microsoft was the lead commercial participant and provided software tools; Education Exchange (Edex) provided the network and Internet connectivity; Mast Learning Systems (MLS) were initially the project managers and were to maintain the ConnectEd Web site; and Guildford College provided the initial training.

Aims and outcomes

17. The aims of the project were to explore the educational benefits of using the Internet; to encourage the development of curriculum-support materials and make them available to others via a network; to explore best-practice examples for sharing resources and curriculum-support materials via a network; to encourage the use of IT as a learning aid by teachers, pupils and parents; and to develop key information-presentation skills in teachers and pupils.

18. The early months of the project were characterised by problems in establishing connectivity. Most schools were not active until the autumn term. While there were some developments in individual schools, there was little communication among them and no sense of a collective project. Consequently, in November 1996, Microsoft called a meeting to re-launch the project. Edex extended free connectivity to the end of March 1997. Focus groups were established, which met in December and identified the main general aim for the remaining period as being the sharing of curriculum materials, particularly in science, though specific activities such as using the Internet as a resource, video conferencing and e-mail communication would continue to be pursued by individual schools. Also in this period, MLS withdrew from the project and Guildford College took over the maintenance of the ConnectEd Web site as well as a leading role in moving the project forward.

19. By the end of the project, connectivity had still not been achieved in two schools, mainly because of incompatibility between their LANs and the requirements for connectivity. The majority of the remainder have 64Kbps access; seven active schools or colleges have 2Mbps access. Networked hardware and its locations are extremely variable, ranging from one Archimedes in an IT classroom to 40 486s and Pentiums dispersed across curriculum areas. More typical is between 10 and 20 machines, the majority located in a library, open-access area, learning resource area or IT suite.

20. Initial training for teachers was provided by Guildford College early in 1996. Although teachers were very positive about the training, most were then frustrated by their inability to practise and develop their skills back in their schools. As indicated above, the subsequent months, which the original timetable had envisaged as being the period of major activity, were dominated by connectivity issues. Thus, the cross-institutional activities which had been at the core of the original aims had not been achieved by the end of the project. Nevertheless, there have been interesting and impressive developments in several individual schools as they have developed their own aims. There is beginning to be evidence of the appeal of the Internet to both teachers and pupils as a major information resource. Across the schools, all age ranges and ability levels were represented. All National Curriculum subjects were involved in project activities and, post-16, most A Levels and GNVQs were also active. The most notable achievement is the increase in motivation, reported by teachers, confirmed by the evaluators' observations, and most clearly evidenced by the constant use of the facilities, during the school day and also early in the morning and after school. Many co-ordinators also reported increased motivation among staff, including those with little previous IT involvement.

21. This can best be expressed in terms of the widespread enthusiasm shown by staff and pupils for Internet activity. Most schools are still in the early stages of learning about the possibilities of the Internet and e-mail. Video conferencing is as yet even less explored. Nevertheless, the majority of schools and colleges involved in the project are very keen to continue with the technology, and some have made considerable progress towards integrating ICT into their curriculum programmes.

Costs and cost benefits

22. By the end of the project, nearly all the schools and colleges were exploring ways in which to maintain connectivity at a cost which was bearable. The initial reaction to the high costs quoted by the commercial sponsors for maintaining connectivity at their current levels was to search for alternative strategies. While several participants were able to take part in local consortia of various types to keep costs down, others were considering a reduced connectivity and lower-cost package being marketed by Edex. With only one exception, all the participating schools and colleges were committed to continuing with ICT, within their budget constraints.

Project A2.3: Kent Broadband Learning Project

Description of the project

23. The project involved three schools in the Medway area of Kent. Because of changes in the local cabling plan, the two original schools in the project, an 11–18 secondary comprehensive girls' school and a junior school which was a feeder to the secondary school, did not, as anticipated, have broadband connectivity. The schools were limited initially to dial-up connectivity to the Internet, but later upgraded to ISDN2, which enabled video conferencing. Because of this, a third school, a girls' grammar, was brought into the project at a later stage in the planning cycle. This school initially had a 64Kbps link, later upgraded to 2Mbps, which gave access to a central server for Internet, cable TV and interactive CD-ROM multimedia learning and teaching materials.

24. The project partners were Kent Education Forum, consisting of

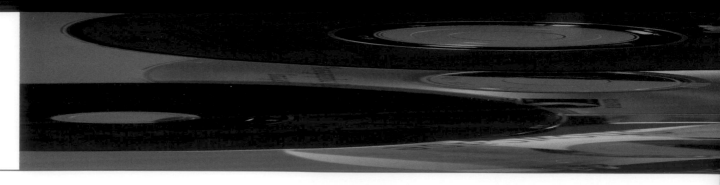

representatives from Kent Training and Enterprise Council (TEC) and Kent Local Education Authority (LEA), United Artists Communications, now Telewest Communications, Research Machines (RM), and BBC Education.

Aims and outcomes

25. The broad aim of the project was to explore the role of ICT in the enhancement of learning. These technologies included broad, intermediate and narrowband access to the Internet and a remote CD-ROM library, as well as video conferencing and cable TV. Further initial aims were to develop links between school and home in order to extend learning opportunities.

26. E-mail links were developed and used highly effectively to support learning in humanities at primary level, and modern languages and English at secondary level. During the lifetime of the project, integration of communications technology into classroom practice and schemes of work was extended across different curriculum areas, and included all age groups. Existing curricular links between the two local schools as part of their transfer arrangements were considerably enhanced by e-mail and video-conferencing exchanges.

27. The girls' grammar school used e-mail to enhance pupils' modern-language skills through an existing multilateral European educational exchange with schools in Holland, Italy, Germany and Finland. Fast Internet access from 16 networked machines catered for class groups to carry out research for coursework within the timetable in sociology and English, thus overcoming the potential inequities of a more common arrangement witnessed elsewhere where pupils only have access to the Net for research purposes outside lesson times.

28. Together, the secondary schools provided a model of how superhighways resources were integrated into pupils' curriculum tasks through careful planning within schemes of work in English, modern languages, media studies and sociology, which ensured progression in ICT and study skills.

29. The success of this project stems from its foundation within already functional educational links, and its continued survival was heavily dependent on the commitment of the schools' project co-ordinators. Many of the junior school's achievements were the result of teachers and pupils working together in learning and developing ICT skills.

30. The project is continuing, and there will be further curricular permeation within the secondary schools and extension of international links. In one of the secondary schools, certain staff have been given specific responsibility for developing ICT within their curriculum area. In the other, a research group has been set up to encourage further staff involvement and extension into other curriculum areas.

31. The project demonstrated that schools can develop their facilities with limited external resources and enterprising use of school budgets, combined with funds from, for example, European projects, bid for on the strength of the schools' communications capabilities. Its success results from the determination and commitment of the schools' project co-ordinators, and its foundation within the schools' pre-existing educational links, such as the cross-phase liaison between two of the schools, and the European modern languages exchange in the third.

32. The Kent Broadband Learning project represents a very successful project which has met its primary aim to explore the role of broad, intermediate and narrow band access to ICT. Despite early difficulties and delays, and, in two of the schools, narrowband access for the first half of the project, a great deal was learned and achieved through the variety of uses explored with each of the communications technologies. A second aim, to develop relationships between educational and commercial partners, was partially achieved, in that existing links between two of the schools were strengthened. At a managerial level, collaboration between all three schools worked well, and their relationship with the Kent LEA developed positively during the project. All of the various players are very keen to develop and extend the project.

33. A third aim, to develop links between school and home in order to extend the opportunities for learning and for staff development, had not been fully explored by the end of the project. Some senior managers had been provided with laptops and modems enabling them to link from home to the school, and a number of pupils with special educational needs were also being provided with computers with Internet and e-mail access. While these initiatives looked likely to develop, it was too early to identify specific outcomes.

Costs and cost benefits

34. Beyond a small setting-up fund, no external funding was made available for the project. Supplemented by sponsorship and/or 'gifts' from commercial providers and manufacturers, the schools themselves invested considerably in extending and upgrading their ICT facilities. One secondary school matched Government funding as a

result of achieving Technology College status and was consequently able to expand networked access.

35. The project showed that small-scale beginnings with dial-up access can represent a relatively cheap and viable option for schools who wish to make the first steps in getting on line. However, where this may be a strategy for start-up initiatives, it is not a feasible solution for integration of ICT across a school or group of schools. Following initial successes, once schools had identified the benefits of faster connectivity and/or increased access, they were committed to seek funds to expand and upgrade their facilities.

Project A2.4: Birmingham Knowledge Superhighways Project

Description of the project

36. The project involved six secondary schools in south Birmingham, three of which were single-sex institutions, two boys-only and one girls-only.

37. Each school had one PC upgraded to enable point-to-point desktop video conferencing. In addition, three of the schools had modem Internet access via a commercial Internet service provider (ISP). Connectivity for video conferencing was via BT ISDN2, supplemented by dial-up/telephone line Internet access.

38. The main focus of the project was video conferencing, although some of the schools also had access to the Internet to support research. A trial of open integrated learning systems (OILS) software in English, maths and modern languages aimed to examine its potential to help raise motivation and achievement. A further aim of the project was to establish home-school links via the

local cable network to support out-of-school learning and out-of-school use of ILS.

39. The main partners were Systems Integrated Research (SIR) and ICL, who provided technical rather than financial support. The project management team was in negotiation with the local cable company to initiate the setting up of a schools' intranet. These discussions were not concluded during the period of the trial and schools continued to use ISDN connectivity.

Aims and outcomes

40. The project sought to explore the potential of intermediate and broadband communications technology for raising pupil achievement, for enhancing the curriculum, and for improving the quality of teaching. An overall objective was to further develop existing collaboration between the schools.

41. The project was subject to technical and organisational problems for the duration of most of the trial. These difficulties seriously hampered progress for four of the six schools, and one of the schools effectively pulled out midway through the trial. Initial inter-school activities designed to get the project started were only partially successful. Although a number of inter-school projects were achieved during the trial, these were, in the main, limited in both number and scope. Further activities were in the planning stage, or were just beginning, at the end of the trial.

42. In addition to video conferencing, two schools developed various initiatives using e-mail and Internet resources, and created school Web sites. Existing video-conferencing links between the girls-only school and a local junior school, which has

a reputation for highly innovative ICT work, have been strengthened during the project, and new contacts with international schools established.

43. The most successful activities arose from a school need, rather than being created specifically for the project. Teachers clearly felt that such school-based initiatives were essential if the project was to move forward. The more active schools also sought links with schools outside the project group. One school in particular remained very active throughout the trial, although many of its activities were not directly related to the project. With the exception of this school, the OILS systems did not feature greatly in the schools' activities and, in general, were not very highly regarded. However, in one school with a Special Learning Unit, the targeted use of specific elements of the English program was reported to have a significant impact on the progress of pupils.

44. The project cannot be said to have fully met any of its aims and objectives. Despite existing links between the schools, there was little collaboration between them during the trial, although there were pockets of successful activity. A single video-conferencing facility seemed to be insufficient to fully involve or enthuse other staff and, in retrospect, a stronger emphasis on the use of the Internet might have been more successful. Because of the failure to reach agreement with the cable company, home-school links were not achieved.

45. The project is still, in effect, in the initial phase, with some useful experiences gained, and a considerable range of projects planned or recently started following the resolution of the various problems. The overall feeling of the

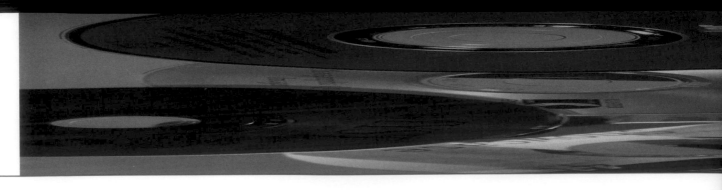

headteachers and teachers was one of disappointment at a lost, rather than a wasted, opportunity and optimism remains fairly high in at least four of the six schools that the project can be re-launched.

Costs and cost benefits

46. Little financial or technical support was available for the project, and it was clear that this situation was not anticipated by some of the schools. The lack of such support clearly contributed to the inability of the schools to resolve the various technical and/or organisational difficulties. For those schools where these dominated, project activity, and thus educational benefits, were negligible, and over the group of schools as a whole, gains were more potential than actual. With one or two exceptions, the schools were reluctant to fund ICT provision without clear evidence that it would be of educational benefit.

Project A2.5: Journeys through Space and Time, now the Rosendale Odyssey

Description of the project

47. Journeys Through Space and Time was a collaboration between Rosendale Infants School, south London, three artists in residence and staff from the Photographers' Gallery. The project was funded by the Sir John Cass Foundation, the Gulbenkian Foundation and the Walcott Educational Charity. Additional sponsorship in the form of equipment and technical help was provided by Kodak and the Arts Technology Centre (Artec).

Aims and outcomes

48. The main aims of the project were to create the opportunity for young children to produce an interactive multimedia program for distribution across the Internet and thereby to establish direct links with other primary school children both nationally and internationally.

49. The main software used was Photoshop, an image manipulation program, and HyperStudio, a multimedia authoring tool specifically designed for use by young children.

50. The project has met most of its aims in full. To date, over half the school's pupils have gained hands-on experience and the work with Year 2 pupils has now been extended into the reception class. Pupils' work done during the school year 1995-96 has been mounted on the school's Web site and has been publicly exhibited at the Photographers' Gallery.

51. Parents and teachers reported that improvements in basic literacy have resulted from the project, and levels of motivation and time on task were observed to have increased.

52. Although there were some initial tensions between teachers and the artists over ways of working, these were speedily resolved and the confidence of the teachers rapidly improved with in-house training to the point where the school's IT co-ordinator now has full responsibility for implementing the programme, including training. The main constraints on further progress have been the limited number of computers, which are housed in the library area. Future plans include having a networked computer in every classroom.

53. The most effective use of the software has been within the context of cross-curricular activity, although the reception class is creating its own literacy project. As pupils have gained in confidence, the teacher's scope for whole-class teaching has decreased, since pupil motivation appears highest when children are encouraged to pursue their own lines of enquiry. This results in an increasing degree of differentiation, requiring individual or group responses from the teacher.

54. The school will amalgamate with the Juniors in the autumn of 1997 and plans are in hand to deploy the new technology to all pupils in both schools. E-mail links with other schools will be extended so that, in the headteacher's words, 'children will learn there is a life beyond the school gates'.

Costs and cost benefits

55. Major capital funding is required to meet the objective of placing one Apple Macintosh computer in each classroom. The pupils include those of African, Caribbean, Asian, Chinese and European descent, and 22 different languages are spoken in the school. In these circumstances, reductions in staff to provide funds to buy more computers are neither educationally desirable nor politically feasible at a time when reductions of at least one member of staff are required to balance the existing budget. No provision has been made for future maintenance.

Project A2.6: Dyfed Satellite Project: Opening the Door to Satellite Remote Sensing

Description of the project

56. The project involved 16 secondary schools, with eventual plans to expand provision to all secondary schools in Carmarthenshire by the end of the 1996-97 academic year. Schools in Ceredigion were to be connected as funds became available. The technology consisted of a network of video-conferencing terminals set up by the Satellite Centre, which also provided Internet

access to schools. By spring 1997, a total of 23 schools (16 in Carmarthenshire, 4 in Ceredigion and 3 in Pembrokeshire) were on line. Four teachers' centres and three administration centres were also involved.

Aims and outcomes

57. The basic project aim was to make the facilities of the Dyfed Satellite Remote Sensing Centre more accessible to teachers and pupils through the use of personal video-conferencing facilities to enhance the IT skills of all staff and some pupils; to meet specific curriculum objectives in A-Level geography; and to develop communication skills and help to increase the social skills of pupils with special needs. Connectivity was via ISDN, installed free of charge by West Wales TEC.

58. The schools have made different rates of progress. This ranged from the least advanced, which experienced considerable technical problems that sapped teachers' initial enthusiasm, to the most advanced which extended the project into curriculum areas other than geography, employed a network manager and produced a development plan which specifically addressed the expansion of ICT.

59. The A-Level geography objectives were met through a series of modules in which small groups of students received remote tutoring from an expert based at the Satellite Centre. The link facilitated shared drawing of diagrams, maps and satellite images, and access to live and archived satellite images. The Centre provided remote INSET for teachers using both point-to-point and multi-point video conferencing. The link has also been used successfully to supplement or to provide teaching in modern languages, GNVQ IT and electronics,

and A-Level psychology and sociology, where staff expertise in some subjects was not available, a factor which potentially limits curriculum breadth in isolated rural secondary schools.

60. The most developed use has been the special needs inter-school video conferences in which pupils with special needs regularly interact with counterparts in other project schools. Pupils progressively developed their conversational skills such as listening, turn-taking and speaking. They gained in social competence and were articulate about the use and value of the exchanges. The success of these links resulted in part from the greater flexibility of their timetables, since a major difficulty in developing video conferencing is the need to pre-arrange conference times within the constraints of secondary school timetables.

61. Internet use was developed further in some schools than others. Access tended to be restricted to sixth-form pupils, and was available at lunch-times for personal research, as opposed to being integral to lessons.

62. The development of staff IT skills has been more successful in the target curriculum areas and with special needs staff, but permeation to staff in other curriculum areas is limited in most schools. The critical factor here, apart from technical problems, is teachers' lack of time for hands-on practice and opportunity to discover resources relevant to their disciplines.

63. There is awareness of the potential of the video link, which can permit multi-point conferencing for headteachers' and co-ordinators' meetings, but this has not been implemented, partly because of technical difficulties. In this rural area with long inter-school distances, the potential exists to use video

conferencing for initial teacher training and continuing professional development group sessions, and for remote support and guidance from their university-based tutors. Cross-phase contact for pupils in small rural feeder primary schools with their secondary schools has been demonstrated through a geography link-up involving the Satellite Centre, and this has considerable potential to ease cross-phase transition when the planned access for primary schools is implemented.

64. The project was generally successful in meeting the aims of enhancing curriculum activity, chiefly in geography, via remote tutoring and access to satellite images, identifying and training senior personnel and providing technical support. It further succeeded in another aim, to provide Internet access to schools. Additional objectives identified by the schools themselves were also being achieved, particularly in special needs education, but also in other curriculum areas such as social sciences, modern languages and business studies. Cross-phase interaction between schools was being explored.

65. The project also fulfilled its aim to be cost effective, and there was considerable potential for the expansion of the Centre's services for schools in both the primary and secondary sectors. A key feature contributing to the success of the project was the role of the project director, whose initiation of the project anticipated the need for senior management involvement, curriculum-based objectives and training, and the need for continuing consultation with project co-ordinators.

Costs and cost benefits

66. Participating schools paid 50% of the costs of equipment and software,

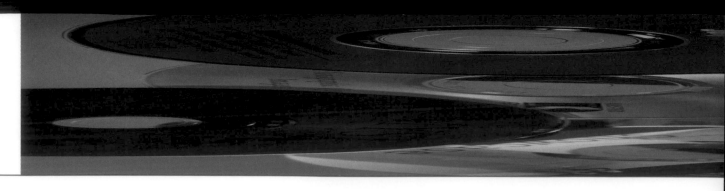

and for on-line charges and rental. The remainder was met through a mix of locally and centrally-provided education grants. The Centre acted as an Internet service provider (ISP) for schools within their full service-level agreements and, although costs of INSET modules were extra, they were at an affordable rate. For this group of small, rural secondary schools, the opportunities to enhance and broaden the curriculum via remote tutoring was a considerable incentive. The costs to schools, already relatively low, were thus offset by savings of travel and supply cover costs. The project was therefore extremely cost effective.

Project A2.7: Powys Access for Schools Project (PACCS)

Description of the project

67. The project provided on-line access to locally created resources through the Rural Wales Wide Area Network (known as RWN). These included geographical, archaeological, archival and fine art materials which were supplied by the Powys Archives Service (PAS), the Clwyd-Powys Archaeological Trust (CPAT) and the 'Artists in Wales' project under the guidance of the Powys Education Authority's Art and Technical Advisor. The co-ordinator of the project was the Powys Education Authority's IT Advisory Officer.

68. Five schools participated in the project, three primary, one secondary and a residential special school, which were all located in sparsely-populated rural areas. The primary schools varied in size between 71 and 285 pupils. One of the schools was bilingual, while the other two taught solely through the medium of English. Each catered for Key Stage 1 and 2 pupils. The secondary school was also bilingual and had 270 students on roll, spanning KS3 and 4.

The special school took its 50 pupils from a wide catchment area and covered KS2 to 4.

Aims and outcomes

69. The main aims of the project were to gather information about harnessing the potential of the Web for converting public resources into educational resources. In pursuit of this aim, it was hoped to promote co-operation between participants and to allow schools increasing access to on-line information. These aims were to be achieved by encouraging public sector bodies to become quality information providers and by enabling pupils themselves to become information providers as well as consumers.

70. Three of the five schools were linked to the RWN via BT ISDN2 lines. Internet access was available through the server based at County Hall. The smallest primary school and the special school had dial-up access to the Internet via BT CampusWorld.

71. Most of the aims of the project were not met because of persistent technical difficulties which occurred throughout the lifetime of the initiative. The limited resources required the project co-ordinator to use most of his available time in remedying faults in the system, with a consequence that there has been little opportunity to follow up initial training with in-school sessions, nor to bring the partners together to share ideas and engage in forward planning. As a result, many of the teachers and the information providers were unclear about the project's aims and were unaware of the identity or activities of the other partners.

72. Despite a lack of collaborative activity among the partner schools, some have taken part in projects originating in other parts of the

United Kingdom or abroad. These provided valuable insights into the potential benefits of the technology for learners, particularly those with special needs, and alerted other less committed teachers to the capacity of the medium to improve levels of pupil motivation.

73. Schools and providers have retained their enthusiasm for the project despite the difficulties they have experienced. The new technology is seen as a key element in broadening the learning experiences of pupils in isolated rural areas and it also has possibilities as an administrative tool. This latter use is dependent on the local authority fostering an 'administrative climate' which encourages the use of electronic communication.

74. The project suffered from a lack of co-ordination, even given the difficulties encountered. If the project is to succeed in the future, there is an urgent need to address the concerns of schools that they lacked any sense of belonging to a project, by establishing a steering group. This group would arrange meetings of representatives, inform schools of any likely developments and be a forum for sharing ideas through newsletters and by use of the telecommunication facilities.

Costs and cost benefits

75. Funding for the project was limited to a relatively small amount of GEST funding. All participants in the project expressed concern about the lack of financial support. Although the schools received free Internet facilities during the trial, it was not possible to judge whether the level of their commitment would remain as high if the project became fully self-funding. Given the local nature of the initiative, and the isolated situation of the schools, it has somewhat restricted relevance in

commercial terms, and sponsorship would not appear to be a viable option. The education authority was committed to the project's continuation but found difficulty in providing support in the face of other financial priorities.

Cross-Project Observations and Recommendations

Value of educationally-defined objectives

76. Initiatives were most successful where schools identified curriculum/professional development objectives and sought technological solutions, rather than introducing the technology and seeking 'problems to solve'.

Teachers' professional development

77. At the time of writing, the Teacher Training Agency (TTA) is undertaking a national survey examining the role of IT in initial teacher training and a consultation exercise on the future of INSET funding. Account should be taken within these TTA initiatives of the likely impact on teaching of ICT. For example, ICT has the potential to facilitate initial teacher training, particularly during school placements. In two projects, effective use was made of video conferencing for remote tutoring of student teachers, and although we saw no specific instances of e-mail being used in this way, there are clear opportunities here also. Such developments may be particularly important for teachers in rural areas.

78. Although the projects in Group A were not specifically concerned with initial teacher training, there was some evidence that many student teachers' levels of IT skills and understanding were weak, and that this was of concern to many schools. The current consultation

documents for a National Curriculum for Teacher Training do not address the issue of new technology beyond the specific requirements of basic IT competence, neither do they examine the wider educational implications of communications technology. It is vital, therefore, that the potential of ICT, both for teaching and as a means of delivering teacher-training programmes, is fully recognised and incorporated into the finalised version of the initial teacher-training curriculum.

79. For practising teachers, effective use was also made of video conferencing, for example for the remote delivery of INSET, often on a on-to-one basis and tailored to an individual teacher's need. Teachers were also able to gain access, and in some cases contribute, to materials on the WWW and on dedicated teachers' resource sites, and to use e-mail and shared areas, such as bulletin boards, to exchange ideas and experiences. Some teachers were beginning to investigate the potential of portable computers, which gave them home-based access to such facilities.

80. While many of these initiatives were at the exploratory stage, communications technology clearly offers tremendous potential for enhancing teachers' professional development, both on an informal, teacher-to-teacher basis, and within more structured programmes. In this, we accord with the conclusions of the recently published Stevenson Report (Stevenson, D., *Information and Communications Technology in UK Schools: An Independent Inquiry*, The Independent ICT in Schools Commission 1996-97) that full account of ICT should be taken within both in-service and initial teacher-training programmes.

Inter-school support

81. ICT offers clear potential for local schools to communicate and work together. However, the contemporary culture of schools is not conducive to co-operation, so that schools with expertise in the use of broadband technology may be unlikely to share their experience with nearby schools. There were notable exceptions, however, particularly where schools already had a history of working collaboratively. This was especially, although not exclusively, true of schools in rural areas.

Administration and inter-school exchanges

82. The projects in Group A were mainly concerned with aspects of curriculum use rather than easing administrative procedures, and the evaluation period was not sufficiently long for the emergence of major developments in this area. An interesting development, however, was the use of ICT to facilitate transfer procedures, for example by the electronic exchange of documentation such as records of achievement, for the monitoring of particular pupils or groups of pupils (including those with special educational needs) between feeder and transfer schools, and to support greater curriculum continuity within transfer (see paragraph 96). There were also numerous examples of exchanges between primary and secondary pupils, and between secondary teachers and primary children, and there is clearly considerable potential in this area.

Careful planning before implementation

83. This points to a need for a thorough consultation and planning phase prior to the initiation of a project.

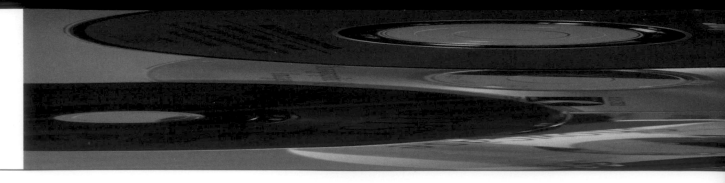

This process should include:

- the clear identification of curricular and/or professional developmental objectives
- careful consideration of the type, level and location of ICT required to meet those objectives
- consideration of the training requirements of staff, including relevant support staff, and pupils
- the setting up of a well-defined and accountable management/co-ordination structure
- the identification and allocation of adequate technical support
- the development of a medium-term plan to carry the initiative beyond the start-up phase.

Avoiding educational and commercial culture clash

84. In some projects, particularly those which were large scale, there was evidence of tension between the educational and commercial partners. To avoid this conflict of cultures, there is a need for a partnership approach, each recognising the distinct contribution the other has to make.

Role of intermediaries

85. This process was enhanced in some projects by the involvement of an intermediary or 'honest broker' with expertise in the educational applications of ICT and a sound knowledge of the culture of schools.

Value of context-based training

86. Similarly, training procedures were most useful where the focus was on context-based exploration of the technology, rather than just skill acquisition. The involvement, in some projects, of experts in the educational as well as technical application of ICT was very effective.

Role of project co-ordinators

87. The role of the project co-ordinator

within the school is crucial. Teachers who took on this role experienced a considerable shift in responsibility and status, particularly in the larger-scale projects. Co-ordinators were most effective where they had a clearly-defined function, and at least the explicit support and involvement of senior management.

Effects on teaching styles

88. While, in general, teachers reported little direct impact on teaching style as a result of the introduction of ICT, the use of the Internet, in particular, has the potential to shift the role of the teacher from instructor to facilitator, helping pupils to search efficiently, critically review the information obtained, and support and develop pupils' problem-solving strategies. While most teachers welcomed this development, and this included previously technophobic teachers who were converted to the use of IT through exposure to the superhighways, some found it threatening.

Cross-curricularity

89. Use of ICT as a learning resource can challenge the traditional discrete subject organisation of the curriculum. Information from the Net, or 'live' information through e-mail, is not always packaged into 'geography' or 'science' parcels but is cross-curricular in content. Whilst primary schools are used to working with cross-curricular topics, the National Curriculum encourages subject compartmentalisation. This is not to say, however, that the existence of subject-based departments in secondary schools necessarily limits the learning potential of the resource, but that ICT offers the potential to work in new ways.

Effects on learners

90. Access to the resources available via the WWW, and the ability to work directly with other schools and agencies via e-mail and video conferencing has considerably enhanced the educational experience of many pupils. In exploring these facilities, pupils have developed high levels of computer and networking skills.

91. There were numerous examples of improvement in pupils' work. This occurred both in structured situations, where the pupils were directed towards materials and activities by the teacher, and in individual access to the technology.

92. A major impact of the projects on pupils was increased motivation and confidence. The 'levelling effect' of ICT was also marked. In many schools, both boys and girls of all ages, academic abilities and backgrounds displayed equal and high levels of expertise, and willingly and confidently shared and discussed their skills and knowledge with others, including their teachers.

93. Equally important was the ability of the new technology to expose pupils to a wider world and, therefore, to develop greater awareness of other cultures. This is particularly timely in the light of the concern currently being expressed about the role of schools in transmitting moral values and good citizenship.

Learners with special educational needs

94. One of the key successes has been the benefits ICT has brought to disenfranchised learners, both pupils with learning difficulties and also the gifted. For pupils with special educational needs, emotional and behavioural difficulties or poor social skills, confidence and self-

esteem were raised, communication skills developed and engagement with their studies increased. For gifted pupils, the opportunities opened up by the Internet have allowed them to explore ideas in ways which would have been very difficult within the classroom context.

Peer tutoring

95. The introduction of peer tutoring, mainly, but not exclusively observed in primary schools, is an exciting development, and has had many direct and positive effects. The 'computer tutors' gained in confidence and self-esteem, children enjoyed being taught by their peers 'in their own language', and teachers were released from much of the routine and repetitive instruction in basic skills.

Cross–phase liaison for easing school transfer

96. Exchanges between schools in different districts or countries has helped to raise pupils' cultural awareness. There have been a number of examples of primary/secondary exchanges for peer-peer tutoring and for joint curriculum projects. The potential for easing the transition between the two when pupils move up to secondary school is considerable.

97. There was a concern in some projects about continuity and progression for highly computer-literate primary school children, who transfer to a secondary school where IT provision is limited, and low levels of skill on entry are assumed.

Raising awareness of primary pupils' IT capabilities

98. The rapid development of expertise in many of the primary schools undermines the view that, in the words of one IT advisory teacher,

'primary schools don't need networks'. Policy makers should give particular consideration to the different, but equally important, needs of the primary sector in planning ICT initiatives.

Distribution and number of workstations

99. During the evaluation, as teachers began to integrate ICT resources into their teaching and learning, the need to provide training for whole classes in basic IT skills was seen as no longer appropriate or necessary. The centralised computer-suite approach is, in our view, less effective than having fewer computers in a greater number of areas, for example in each classroom or subject area. There was evidence that, in schools with a large number of networked workstations, there was a shift towards this more diffused model of distribution.

Protection against exposure to undesirable applications

100. Three major approaches emerged to deal with this issue:

- Protected or 'walled garden' environments were seen as particularly suitable for younger pupils. In some cases, however, 'protection' became increasingly to be seen as 'limitation'.

- Filtered access allowed for access to a wider range of sites, but with some element of control over unsuitable materials. This was regarded as a much more flexible approach, but still caused concern for some teachers since it was possible for young learners to access inappropriate sites.

- While screening mechanisms were generally regarded as appropriate for younger learners, teachers were also concerned to encourage pupils to develop

responsible attitudes coupled with sanctions if trust was breached. The preferred solution here was to provide open access to networks, but to operate close supervision. This approach is, however, potentially time consuming for teachers. What might be called 'virtual surveillance', that is the possibility that searches or e-mails might be monitored, acted as a powerful deterrent.

Technical reliability

101. Technical problems, particularly unreliable connectivity or lack of compatibility, were responsible for a loss of commitment and enthusiasm in some initiatives. Technical systems require technical experts to ensure their proper installation and continuing maintenance and, in many of the projects, this was simply unavailable or beyond the means of school budgets. The role of technical support would normally be assumed by the LEA but, in the present climate, this is often no longer financially feasible.

102. Some schools were considering the possibility of sharing technical support personnel, for example between a secondary school and its primary feeder. The joint financing of such support through a local federation of schools or through partnerships with the LEA, TECs or local businesses, is suggested as a possible way forward.

Creating productive networks

103. There is clear potential for creating productive networks at a local level, although the contemporary culture of schools is not conducive to co-operation. The strongest links were forged between schools which were not in competition for pupils. In particular, relationships between primary feeder schools and their

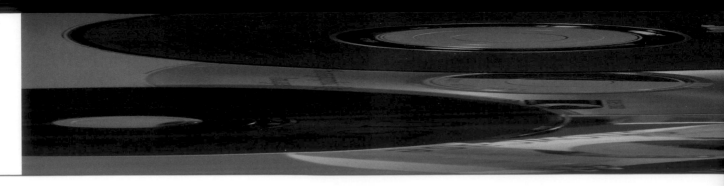

related secondary schools were enhanced by a sharing of the technology. Some schools and colleges also forged links with local groups, such as TECs, businesses, universities and LEAs, to generate the funds to continue connectivity.

104. While there is a real concern about the issue of competition, it is also recognised that ICT enables communication with institutions that are outside a school's immediate area. There were a number of examples of productive co-operation at national and international level. These tended to build on existing links, however, and, in the absence of any kind of directory, there were difficulties in developing new relationships.

Data speed

105. Schools with narrowband access rather than faster connectivity experienced considerable delays which proved to be frustrating and off-putting. However, many of the main delays occurred as the result of heavy traffic elsewhere so that, for example, schools were often frustrated in the afternoon when attempting to use the Internet, irrespective of the nature of their connectivity.

106. The importance of speed is directly related to the importance of the technology required to meet the curriculum or professional development needs of the school. Some schools were convinced that 'starting small' with narrowband access was a viable option. Nevertheless, these schools understood the value of wider-band access, and progressed towards higher-capacity connectivity as far and as quickly as resources allowed.

107. In general, therefore, the aim should be to achieve connectivity at the broadest width possible, budgeting for costs to anticipate future developments in superhighways technology.

Costs and cost benefits

108. Difficulties arose in arriving at accurate costings because of the complex ways in which the various projects were funded, and in some cases subsidised. At its simplest, a school with available cabling and a willingness to transfer its telephone account to the cabling company has almost no start-up costs other than the staff time required for implementation, assuming that the cost of technical support and maintenance and of appropriate hardware and software can be met within existing budgets.

109. The projects in Group A were very varied, allowing for comparisons between different models of implementation, from a fully-managed networked service across a group of schools, for example BEON, to a single school working with just two stand-alone computers at Rosendale. These are discussed in the main body of the cross-project report (see Report A3).

110. In general, our observations indicate that large-scale funded projects benefited considerably from guaranteed commercial expertise and expert technical support. However, the real costs of such services, once sponsorship was removed from the equation, were beyond most schools. Nevertheless, even in the smaller-scale initiatives, once the potentiality of the system had been demonstrated, demand for additional ICT resources increased rapidly. Most primary schools argued for at least one networked machine per classroom. At secondary schools, the equivalent would be at least one fully-equipped laboratory within the major curriculum areas. The educational potential of ICT has been clearly demonstrated in all of the projects, regardless of scale.

111. The need for accessible technical expertise was revealed in most of the Group A projects, not only after installation but from the planning stage, given that most schools will have to achieve compatibility between an existing and any new facility, for example as in Project ConnectEd. Secondary schools, therefore, may be able to budget for a network manager. For primary schools, the possibility of forming consortia with other primary schools and/or a local secondary school should be considered as a means of making such essential support affordable, if LEA services cannot be used.

112. Currently, the lowest quoted commercial costs for a basic managed service varied between the cost of one-and-a-half teachers' salaries per annum in the primary school, and four-and-a-half in the secondary schools. In the present climate, where schools are already facing the possibility of severe cuts in staffing, no school in the project was able to contemplate such additional expenditure without outside sponsorship. Since, clearly, not all schools could secure this, a nationally-funded initiative will be necessary if widespread connectivity is to be achieved.

Group S
Curriculum Projects in Scotland
Executive Summary

The Projects

1. This report describes the findings of an evaluation carried out by the Scottish Council for Research in Education (SCRE) of two Scottish projects included in the four UK Education Departments' Superhighways Initiative (EDSI). The two projects were Modern Communications for Teaching and Learning in Argyll and Bute and Superhighways Teams Across Rural Schools (STARS). The evaluation was managed by the Scottish Council for Educational Technology (SCET) for the Scottish Office Education and Industry Department (SOEID), and ran from January 1996 to March 1997.

Project S2.1: Modern Communications for Teaching and Learning in Argyll and Bute

Description of the project

2. The evaluation was of ongoing work in Argyll and Bute Council to develop an electronic communications network for educational purposes. The network had been in existence for some four years before the evaluation began, and staff in schools and in the Education Development and Support Unit (EDSU) were actively engaged in explorations of the most appropriate ways to make use of the network to enhance the curriculum, to extend opportunities for teaching and learning, and to support the management of schools and co-operatives (cluster groups of primary schools within a defined geographical area). The evaluation is based on the work of two co-operatives, and focuses on a variety of school-based initiatives making use of telephone, fax, a closed-conference network (Argyll Online) and video communications, which were under way during the evaluation period.

Aims and outcomes

3. The aims of the project were to:

- develop an effective communications policy and strategy within an educational context
- enhance the curriculum
- support staff development in the use of electronic communications technology
- promote interactive teaching and learning
- enhance the personal and social development of pupils and teachers.

4. These are all long-term aims which the Authority did not expect to achieve fully during the evaluation period. However, the evaluators noted progress in all of the aims over this time. Significant outcomes identified in the course of the evaluation are listed under the main headings below, and described in more detail in the report (see Report S2.1).

Development of an effective communications policy and strategy

5. Evaluation showed that there was:

- strong support for this initiative at senior management level
- centralised control of the development of the network
- embedding of the network in the co-operative structure
- a commitment to training for all staff in the Authority
- careful planning, implementation, monitoring and evaluation of innovation
- scope and support for autonomous development within schools and co-operatives.

Curriculum enhancement

6. Outcomes included:

- integration of the use of electronic communications in core subject areas
- specific projects to explore the potential of electronic

communications, for example in teaching modern languages in primary schools, art teaching, and 'bridging' projects designed to support transition of primary school pupils to secondary school

- extensive use of the network by pupils, independently of teachers, when judged appropriate for the task in hand.

Staff development in the use of electronic communications technology

7. Evaluation showed that there was:

- a policy decision that all teachers and all pupils be competent in the use of the various forms of electronic communications available, to prevent the dominating effect of 'experts' and 'technophobes'
- INSET in basic technical skills provided for all teachers by EDSU
- training materials developed by EDSU for staff and pupil use, on the basis of needs identified by teachers, for example easy-to-use training cards
- recognition that training in the use of the technology for teachers and pupils is most successful when delivered in the context of the curriculum.

Interactive teaching and learning

8. Outcomes here included:

- development of a range of curricular activities which are delivered electronically and which support collaboration of pupils and teachers across schools, usually within a co-operative
- a focus on identifying appropriate uses of electronic communications to support the day-to-day work of the class
- development of distance learning approaches for use by specialist teachers.

Enhanced personal and social development

9. Opportunities to make contact outside the school community are particularly important in isolated rural areas because:

   - pupils who may have few or no peers in their own school gain from the chance to collaborate with others in other schools

   - there is an extended audience for shared work, for discussion and development of ideas, which is so important for pupils in small schools

   - teachers, particularly those in one-teacher schools, need opportunities to share experiences, practice and ideas

   - using the network enhances opportunities for teachers' professional development in a variety of other contexts as well as those connected to electronic communications.

Costs and cost benefits

10. The use of electronic communications in Argyll and Bute schools has extended and enhanced the curriculum by enabling teachers to share their expertise in developing core curricular materials. It has encouraged BT and Strathclyde University Faculty of Education to work with the Authority to produce commercial materials. It has also developed distance learning approaches and enabled teachers and pupils to collaborate with peers, collect and share information and to experience learning environments other than the school.

11. For school management, the introduction of video conferencing within co-operatives has not only saved travel costs and time for headteachers, but also encouraged them to set tight agendas and deal with routine matters through fax or e-mail, thereby reducing the number of physical meetings.

Project S2.2: Superhighways Teams Across Rural Schools (STARS)

Description of the project

12. This project, based at Northern College of Education, in Aberdeen and Dundee, was designed to create a network of schools in isolated rural areas across the north and north west of Scotland, with the aim of enhancing provision for able pupils. Eighteen small primary schools, with four teachers or fewer, and two secondary schools took part. The project ran between January and December 1996.

13. The project made use of electronic communications technology which schools already possessed, and Northern College's existing closed-conference system, using FirstClass™ software. Materials for pupil use were developed by the project co-ordinators at Northern College and delivered to schools over the network. All tasks aimed to promote problem-solving and critical and creative thinking skills. Some activities were designed as stand-alone tasks and others required pupils to collaborate across schools before finalising responses and returning these to the project co-ordinators for comment. Pupils communicated via the conference system using e-mail, group conferencing or on-line chat. Towards the end of the project, tasks which required pupils to access information from the Internet were designed for a subset of schools interested in developing skills in this area.

Aims and outcomes

14. The aim of the project was to enhance pupils' learning and the professional development of teachers using existing electronic communications technology. The evaluators were asked to focus on:

   - the extent to which appropriate learning benefits can be provided via an electronic communications network to meet the special needs of isolated able pupils

   - the extent to which different communications technologies can be integrated to deliver relevant and effective training and professional development opportunities

   - the comparative performance of different service and carrier technologies.

15. Significant outcomes in these areas are listed under the main headings below, and addressed in more detail in the body of the report (see Report S2.2).

Appropriate learning benefits for isolated able pupils

16. There was a wide range of benefits for able pupils, including:

   - taking greater responsibility for their own learning

   - increased confidence and enthusiasm

   - opportunity to share ideas with high-ability pupils in other schools

   - new awareness that peers from other schools could out-perform them

   - greater attentiveness to the needs of others in the school and willingness to help them.

   Additionally, there were sometimes unexpected gains for other pupils, including:

   - increased pupil awareness of problem-solving and creative and critical thinking skills and significant development of these skills, applied not only to STARS activities but to other work within the school.

Delivery of training and professional development for teachers via electronic means

17. This included:

- development of a range of technical skills in the use of the conference system and of the Internet, both as a result of hands-on experience and of specific training and support

- opportunities to explore ideas about able pupils and strategies to support them

- opportunities to experience and discuss the effects of a concentrated and overt focus on problem-solving and creative and critical thinking skills.

Performance of different services and carrier technologies

18. Findings here included:

- FirstClass™ proving reliable and user friendly, although the cost of working on line was a disincentive to extensive use

- difficulties arising from incompatibilities in transferring documents produced using different software packages being resolved by adopting Rich Text Format (RTF) as the standard format for attachments, although this limited the nature of work which could be shared among schools

- uneven access in project schools to telephone and ISDN lines also having an adverse effect on the project's development

- Apple Remote Access software being found not to be an appropriate form of access to the Internet for project schools.

Costs and cost benefits

19. Teachers were convinced of the gains which they and their pupils had made, not only in relation to understanding and applying problem-solving and creative and critical thinking approaches, but also in IT skills. Professional development is feasible through electronic communications and, although it cannot replace face-to-face meetings, it may be a cost-effective approach in areas where it is difficult for teachers to meet at a central location.

Cross-Project Observations and Recommendations

Professional development

20. Effective professional development is crucial to the introduction of information and communications technology (ICT) and should cover both the technical skills required to use the technologies and an understanding of their educational potential. Both projects demonstrate the effectiveness of training that is delivered in the context of the curriculum, allowing teachers to see the educational rationale for, and benefits of, using ICT. In Argyll and Bute, this was reinforced by management structures that facilitated the identification of training needs by staff themselves. The STARS project showed that technical training and support can be delivered electronically, but that this is much enhanced when teachers have the opportunity to discuss new educational ideas and develop approaches collaboratively.

Small schools in remote rural areas

21. The potential benefits to be gained from electronic communications technologies by small schools in remote rural areas are considerable. It has, traditionally, been difficult for such schools to have access to the

range of sources of information and educational opportunities which are commonly available to schools in urban areas. In small schools, pupils and teachers have few or no peers with whom to interact, and opportunities for developing and sharing new ideas, discussing, practising and arguing can be limited. Electronic communications offer a variety of solutions to these problems and schools in the two projects have been inventive in developing the potential of the technologies to which they had access.

Teaching and learning

22. To become effective tools for teaching and learning, electronic communications need to be integrated into the daily work of the class. Work in Argyll and Bute has focused on developing materials and approaches which support the integration of electronic communications technologies into the 5–14 curriculum, and on encouraging teachers and pupils to identify the most appropriate uses of the various electronic methods available for particular tasks. The STARS project has demonstrated that particular learning approaches using problem solving, and critical and creative thinking, which are encouraged in 5–14 and which teachers are keen to introduce and develop with their pupils, can be promoted effectively via electronic communications.

23. Both projects have also highlighted the fact that technical training and development for teachers and pupils are most effective when delivered in the context of the curriculum.

Use of the fax

24. The fax machine has proved to have unexpected potential for schools. It

is widely used by pupils and teachers in Argyll and Bute classrooms to make contact with other schools to request information, to enable pupils to collaborate across schools on activities such as surveys or story writing, and to make arrangements to make contact using other forms of electronic communication, for example video communication.

School management

25. Aspects of school and co-operative management, particularly in rural areas, can be achieved more efficiently through electronic communications. In Argyll and Bute, video conferencing has proved valuable not only in reducing travel time for managers who previously met face-to-face on a regular basis, but has also led to other efficiency gains. For example, awareness of 'on-air' costs has encouraged managers to deal with routine issues by fax or e-mail before video meetings take place, thus reducing the overall length of time spent in meetings.

Network structures

26. The establishment of a human network is a key prerequisite for an electronic network. The co-operative structure introduced in Argyll and Bute at approximately the same time as the electronic network has been a significant factor in the success of the development of the Authority's electronic communications strategy. It created a motive for communication and a natural focus for the introduction of a range of innovations, several of which have focused on the development of a common approach to 5–14. At the same time, the co-operative structure has benefited considerably from the ease of communications and the scope for collaboration which electronic communications have provided. The two networks, the human and the electronic, are now closely interlinked.

Access and equity

27. The 'market forces' approach to developing an infrastructure for electronic communications in the UK has not led to an equitable distribution of resources for schools. Neither project had access to broadband technology. While both have achieved much using narrowband (ordinary telephone lines), and, to a limited extent, intermediate technology (ISDN lines), and have demonstrated the fact that small schools in isolated rural areas can benefit from electronic communications, possibly to a greater extent than larger schools in urban areas, the absence of broadband technology in rural Scotland, and of the opportunities which could be made available via broadband, is a limiting factor and will continue to be so.

28. Furthermore, funding to support the introduction and development of electronic communications in small schools needs to be reviewed. While Argyll and Bute has been highly successful in securing commercial sponsorship to support the development of its network and, as a single authority, has been able to control the cost of using the network for individual schools, some schools in the STARS project were handicapped by insufficient access to computers, telephone points and telephone lines and by the cost of calls. What would, for a larger school, constitute relatively insignificant additional expense, can represent a large proportion of the budget of a school with only a few hundred pounds a year to spend after allocated costs are met.

Partnerships between industry and educational institutions

29. Both projects demonstrated that industry can benefit from partnerships with educational institutions. In Argyll and Bute, partnership with BT has produced a number of developments which are of benefit to industry, for example the development of video-conferencing protocols, but other curricular work and training materials and approaches developed independently by both projects have wider applications. It would be to the advantage of commercial organisations to seek to develop closer links with schools and other educational institutions engaged in developing applications of electronic communications technology for educational purposes.

Costs and cost effectiveness

30. Individual schools will find it difficult or impossible to take responsibility for the full costs of involvement in electronic communications networks. Small schools in particular are likely to be disadvantaged if support from education authorities, commercial sponsors or other agencies is not available.

31. The two projects involved in the evaluation adopted very different approaches to funding. In Argyll and Bute, the Authority instigated the project, and decisions about levels of resourcing were taken centrally. The Authority was also responsible for seeking commercial sponsorship to support the development of the network and for drawing up a model of financial support in which some costs were eventually devolved to schools when the educational value of the technology had been demonstrated.

32. In the STARS project, the aim was to make use of schools' existing resources. From the evaluation, it is clear that such models, while undoubtedly attractive, require careful auditing of the resources available to participants at the

outset – including time for training, co-ordination and support, and provision for some upgrading – in order for the newly-formed network to function effectively.

33. It should be noted that clear evidence of cost effectiveness is unlikely to be immediately available in the case of projects initiating and developing experimental work with new technologies. Those setting up such projects would benefit from establishing 'benchmark' costs in areas where savings are eventually anticipated, as these are difficult to retrieve retrospectively.

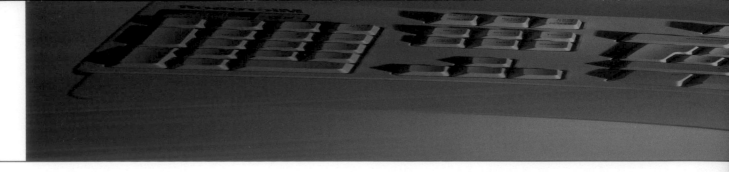

improve and this has been particularly so where INSET courses have been arranged. The project has received recognition at local and national level, and this has succeeded in raising the profile of Burnley College amongst the community, and recruitment from the schools involved in the project has increased by over 50% since the project started. The Telematics Certificate, which was developed as a method of monitoring usage and competency of the video-conferencing facilities, has received considerable recognition, so much so that a further 30 institutions will soon be franchised to operate it, using the materials developed.

Project B2.5: London Colleges Multimedia Initiative

Description of the project

46. The London Colleges Multimedia Initiative is a large and complex project with many partners based on a confederation of the Greater London Training and Enterprise Councils (TECs) and 22 colleges funded by the Further Education Funding Council (FEFC). The overall project is grouped into four regionally-organised consortia (Central, North, South and West London), formed on the area of influence of one of the sponsoring TECs. The consortia form a loose federation and each individual project within each consortium is autonomous.

47. The initiative began in August 1995, although planning for funding bids had taken place earlier in the year. Subject to continuing funding, which depends upon the attainment of targets, the project will continue for three years. The evaluation covers the initiative during the year February 1996 to February 1997.

48. Each of the 22 college projects is funded from the Government's competitiveness fund, a three-year initiative to encourage and assist FEFC-funded colleges to work together to contribute to improving the region's competitive advantage. Key areas identified as having priority were multimedia, telematics and the information superhighway; the devising, experimenting and exploiting of new ways of teaching and learning; and delivering learning materials telematically.

49. All the colleges have their own internal college networks, with sometimes several networks existing on the same site or across separate sites, and most colleges had connected their academic networks to the superhighway in order to give staff and students access to the Internet and to e-mail facilities.

50. A variety of models of connectivity to the superhighway were in place:
    - a private wide area network (WAN)
    - connection through the University of London Computing Centre (ULCC)
    - connection through to a local university via a BT Megastream connection (2Mbps)
    - connection via microwave link
    - connection through a local cable supplier
    - connection via an ISDN line.

51. The focus of activity has been to increase the competitiveness of business within the region, to improve access to high-quality vocational training, to harness new technologies to improve the flexibility of training provision, and to respond better to the needs of employers and individuals for continuous skills development and lifelong learning. This has involved

the production of teaching and learning materials based upon the new technologies, and the provision of access and flexibility in response to the needs of the local communities, particularly local industry and commerce.

Aims and outcomes

52. The intended outcomes of the initiative are that learners will be able to undertake their studies in more flexible and accessible ways, and utilise to the full their skills of handling and communicating information acquired through their studies. In line with the Government's objective, the initiative will contribute to the goal of ensuring learners are adequately prepared for initiation into or return to working life able to understand and use new technologies.

53. Learners will also have improved access to support, through the flexibility of broadband connectivity, to enable them to have direct and immediate interactive communication to their tutors and other teaching services, together with the facility for on-line assessment and management of learner responses.

54. The specific outcomes sought include:
    - the establishment of an information superhighway as a catalyst for lifelong learning and skills development for the individual, in order to enhance the economic performance of businesses in London
    - the development of broader use of technology for information interchange, and promotion of the use and benefits of the Internet to colleges, schools, businesses and other agencies such as careers service partnerships, employment services and TECs

- support for the National Education and Training Targets through the development of work-based learning systems allowing development through the NVQ Level 3 qualification in priority skills areas

- support for the development of new learning methods, both for colleges and for employers, by using technology to provide open access to vocational skills training

- the promotion of vocational training and qualifications across organisations within the region, encouraging increased investment in future skills development

- the maintenance of current levels of vocational education and training in construction and engineering-based industries

- economic growth through vocational skills development in identified priority areas in both large organisations and small and medium-sized enterprises (SMEs)

- highly cost-effective vocational-training provision within the workplace and within the colleges

- increased access to flexible vocational-training provision in the workplace, for home-based students and in areas of special need.

55. Such a wide range of outcomes will ensure that vocational education and training will contribute significantly to improving competitive advantage in London by their ability to:

- widen access to provision, including particular specialisms within any college

- enrich curriculum content by improved access to resources

- foster more versatile approaches to the development of core skills in both academic and vocational courses

- promote collaborative ventures with the local community,

including employers and schools, and between UK colleges and their counterparts in other countries

- gain access to sources of information on vocational needs to improve the responsiveness of colleges to changing vocational requirements, both in the UK and in Europe

- provide information, advice and guidance to prospective students, especially adults wishing to re-enter education.

56. To a large extent, the main themes of the objectives have been realised in the form of:

- the development of courses targeted at local commerce and industry, specifically addressing training needs in the new technologies

- improved access to courses and learning materials through open learning and the use of the Internet

- using technology for the development of courses for people with severe disabilities and for unemployed people

- production of multimedia learning materials

- in-house development of CD-ROM based learning materials

- staff development linked to the use of technology.

57. All the colleges which were visited organised programmes of staff development which were available to all staff employed by the college. These courses were of three types.

- Introductory awareness training for staff. These courses were generally short, and provided sufficient knowledge and skills to enable self-learning to proceed.

- Specialist training for staff. Staff taking these courses were

encouraged to participate in a variety of ways. Sometimes remission time was given, sometimes overtime was paid. In one college, staff were loaned a high-specification multimedia PC to use at home.

- Organisation of conferences for staff from schools and colleges within or outside the project.

Sponsors

58. Funding for this project has been obtained from the FEFC, the European Social Fund, the SRB and the respective colleges.

Costs and cost benefits

59. The 22 colleges were grouped into four regional consortia in which they could collaborate on the devising of projects to fulfil the broad aims of the London Colleges Multimedia Initiative. Collaboration is the mechanism which enables the colleges to bid for finance through the Government's competitiveness funding programme. Guidance from the Government Office for London indicated that the bids must be collaborative, that funding must be spent in a collaborative way and not shared out between colleges, that employer involvement was essential and that matched funding was the basis for the allocation of any finance. Bids are made annually to and allocated by the London Regional Group which comprises representatives from business, the FEFC, the Government Office for London and the DfEE. Thus, the funding of the specific individual initiatives in this project were often part of an overall scheme within a consortium.

60. As detailed above, the benefits which accrued to the colleges and the local communities were significant, but the multiplicity of

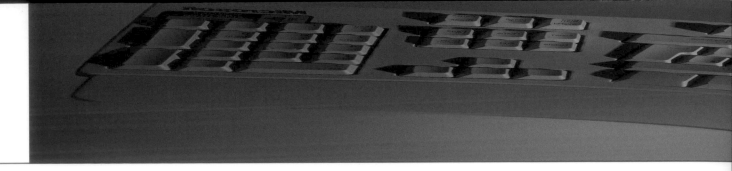

projects, the use of the superhighway for general educational administration was not a feature of any of the projects evaluated. There is, however, clear potential for such usage in terms of asynchronous information exchange and access to shared resources as well as synchronous video conferencing and application sharing.

Cost benefits

120. Benefits which have occurred have been largely in terms of curriculum enhancement, including improvement of access for disabled students and the local community; improvement in attitudes and enthusiasm; development of technical skills; and improved performance levels. It is difficult to quantify in strictly financial terms such individual benefits, let alone the vast developments which have occurred in terms of IT skills amongst the staff, students and pupils who have been involved. All of the projects, to a greater or lesser degree, have shown measurable benefits, but whether or not these justify the costs incurred is essentially a matter of individual opinion. What is notable, though, is that some teaching staff are clearly so convinced of the benefits to learning that they are prepared to commit much additional energy and time to the development of the use of the technology.

Future developments

121. Two of the projects in Group B have now reached the final stage of development. Others have been extended or are in the process of developing into new projects, often depending extensively on the experiences gained during the course of the evaluation. Several projects are now beginning to develop with most interesting proposals for the

future and it is important that this work continues to be closely monitored so that the results may be more widely disseminated.

Group C
Teachers' Professional Development Executive Summary

The Projects

1. Two projects dealing with teachers' professional development were accepted for inclusion in EDSI. These were the CLASS Project in Northern Ireland, and the Teachers Managing Learning (TML) project in Cambridgeshire. These projects contrasted starkly in every respect, as is shown in Table 1 below.

Table 1 A comparison of the CLASS and TML projects

	CLASS	TML
Project leaders	CLASS team	Cambridgeshire LEA team
No. of schools	4	300 in Phase 1, 12 in Phase 2
Superhighways component	Video conferencing	Video conferencing (Internet and WWW)
Focus	Impacting on school management	Impacting on the school curriculum
Sponsors	CLASS, NICLR, ICL, SIMS, BT, RTU, Coopers & Lybrand	LEA (BT minimally) and the County Department of IT
Superhighways role	Means of providing professional development	Subject of professional development

2. The projects as a pair did offer an opportunity to view the potential role of superhighways technology in teachers' professional development, both as a means of delivery and as an agent for change in administrative and curriculum-related aspects of the work of the school. However, it should be noted that these projects only begin to address a small sector of the possible uses of superhighways technologies in the domain of the professional development of teachers. Training of teachers, both in terms of their own use and understanding of superhighways technologies and related issues for use of these technologies in schools, will clearly be essential to the 'roll out' of any successful strategies identified by EDSI.

Project C2.1: CLASS Project

Description of the project

3. The CLASS project explored the application of an interactive multimedia CD-ROM and video conferencing via ISDN2 lines to provide an independent training module in the use of computerised management information systems (CMIS). Four secondary schools in Northern Ireland took part and a total of 28 senior and middle managers engaged in the training programme. The project was successfully completed by a partnership of public and commercial organisations, including the CLASS organisation, NICLR, SIMS, ICL, BT, RTU and Coopers and Lybrand.

4. ICL provided each school and the tutor centre with a Pentium multimedia computer running Windows 3.1 and VC8000 card with Teamvision software on each machine. A Call Port® external audio system was installed after initial system testing. BT installed an ISDN2 line in each school and training centre.

Aims and outcomes

5. All of the aims set by the project team were achieved. In particular, the project was found to provide an efficient and effective platform for flexible in-service provision for the acquisition of skills and knowledge, empowering schools to manage some of their own professional development needs cheaply and with minimum disruption to pupil learning. Other significant organisational benefits for schools were identified, conducive to improvements in the quality and range of influence of school-based decision-making. However, because the aspiration to co-ordinate the delivery of a Windows '95-based upgraded CLASS system in parallel with the EDSI CLASS project was not realised within the evaluation time-scale, it was not possible to observe any improvements in the effectiveness of educational processes in the four schools.

6. There were some significant technical problems, which caused intermediate delays, but were all successfully overcome. This highlighted the need for high-quality technical support when introducing technology-rich training programmes of this kind.

7. The project successfully employed a strongly controlling management strategy, making full use of high levels of motivation among participants and a capability to deliver equipment and support by members of the partnership. Internally, participating schools were encouraged to assume ownership of the training task and to be accountable, through externally administered tests, for its effectiveness. This proved to be a significant contributory factor in the project's success.

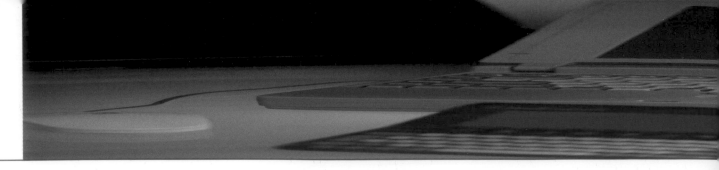

8. A programme of training events revealed that designing multimedia training applications for professional users should, as far as possible, simulate actual operating conditions and be closely relevant to users' practical interests and needs. Hands-on experience should be incorporated in the training programme, which should be provided as close as possible to the time when the system may be actually used in school. Significant opportunities for school development and inter-school networking were identified.

9. The pedagogy adopted in the CD-ROM package was structured around three component procedures, which supported the development of knowledge, the acquisition of skills and further study through a reinforcement-feedback loop. The strategy was further supported by coupling the CD-ROM package to a video-conferencing facility. This facility was used effectively by CLASS for internal project evaluation and testing of trainees in their acquisition of skills and knowledge. The CD-ROM provided an effective teaching environment. All participants successfully completed the training programme and were generally positive about their multimedia learning experiences. The facility's capability to promote staff and organisational development was less fully utilised. A number of insights were obtained regarding necessary conditions for successful training programmes aimed at professionals and using an independent mode of learning, notably in respect of their internal management, the requirements of a satisfactory learning environment and individual patterns of study and learning.

Costs and cost benefits

10. In terms of the efficiency and cost-effectiveness of this independent mode of training, direct savings at the school level, arising from greatly reduced tuition, travel and teacher substitution costs, together with minimum disruption to patterns of pupil learning, make this a highly attractive option. Estimation of the indubitable economies would need a re-examination of the role and nature of in-service training.

11. Qualitatively, teachers highly valued being able to take control of their own learning, especially when so closely related to their specific organisational responsibilities, and this produced an extended training day from 8.00 am to 6.00 pm. Individual learning experiences could then be shared with other colleagues, as part of their collective responsibility for particular organisational tasks. From the school's perspective, the approach was found to promote a more extensive and equal distribution of corporate skills and provided a common platform amongst staff from which to develop a school-based strategy for self-development. Opportunity costs were incurred through teachers engaging in training during school time. Extensive use of this training pattern will require schools to produce a negotiated professional staff development model.

Project C2.2: Teachers Managing Learning Project

Description of the project

12. The Teachers Managing Learning (TML) project in Cambridgeshire involved a collaboration between three LEA agencies and the County Department of Information Technology to provide an opportunity for every school in the authority to have an 'awareness of superhighways technology' training session in which the relevance of these technologies to future school and curriculum development would be aired. There was no charge to schools for attendance at these sessions; the agencies absorbed the considerable cost as they viewed the exercise as one in which they would invest in order to generate new business among their schools as raised awareness led to a need for further staff training. There was an expectation that these sessions would lead to some schools opting to pursue these developments actively, including them in their school development plan and buying in the help of LEA support staff to assist in the related staff and curriculum development which would result. This would then form Phase 2 of the project.

Aims and outcomes

13. The project succeeded in its primary aims to provide all schools with this first-stage training opportunity, which over half the county's schools took up. There was a high degree of satisfaction with the sessions attended, and most schools sent senior management and information technology (IT) specialists. The attendees recognised the value of the largely new information they received, and offered the view that the technologies they experienced would have relevance to their schools in the next five years. These included e-mail, World Wide Web (WWW) access and video conferencing. Moreover, a majority of schools expressed a desire to join the second phase of the project.

14. Phase 2 of TML involved inviting all schools in the county to purchase LEA support for a variety of training and development options relating to the development of teachers' skills in various aspects of superhighways technologies, and their integration into the curriculum. These ranged from using WWW resources in the classroom, through authoring Web pages to using video conferencing.

However, the second phase of the project has yet to take off. Some 12 schools have expressed interest in the opportunities offered, but as yet no firm commitments have been made.

15. It is important to view the TML initiative in the broader context of the county as a whole. Running in Cambridgeshire, in parallel, there have been two initiatives to put an information and communications technology (ICT) facility into every school, and provide free access to the county bulletin board. The County Department of IT runs this service at no charge to the schools. Through it they can use e-mail to handle routine administrative communication within the county, access standard e-mail and have full Internet access. Where schools have a contract with certain local cable companies for their telephone services, calls to the bulletin board are free. Cable service is only available in urban areas of Cambridgeshire. All county schools are now using this service at some level for administration. Thirty-three schools are using it for WWW access. In the case of schools that sent staff to the training sessions, this use has begun since they attended the sessions.

16. The exact impact of a broad-stroke approach to teachers' professional development can be difficult to assess accurately. Certainly, in terms of equity of access to a training opportunity, all schools irrespective of size, location or available budget were given a chance to update themselves on the role of superhighways technologies in schools. There is evidence that some of the schools who did not avail themselves of this opportunity are already active ICT users, via the bulletin board

and in some cases through other service providers. There is, however, no way of knowing how far this use impacts on the curriculum in any of the county's schools.

17. TML Phase 1 is viewed by the LEA staff involved as one component of a broader plan that will have a wide-ranging impact on the county's schools over a period of years. The fact that it has not led to direct impact on curriculum use of superhighways technologies within the time-scale of EDSI has not been surprising for the support staff involved. They are aware that schools work on a medium-term development plan model, with demands on budgets for resources and professional development carefully prioritised and committed at least a year in advance. The lack of response to an immediate offer of development of the use of superhighways technologies must be viewed against this background. There are already indications that some schools wish to pursue this as part of their plan for 1998–99, and to work with the LEA to do this. Interestingly, these are all schools who already have work under way that involves active use of external sources of information in curriculum work, and who wish to improve their methods of access to these sources. There are indications that schools who do not currently actively use communications with organisations or individuals outside the school by more traditional methods are unlikely to rush to do so using superhighways technologies. A view is emerging that 'outward looking' schools who regard the wider community as part of their school's resources are more likely to adopt ICT.

Cross-Project Observations and Recommendations

18. Though attempting primarily to assess the efficiency and effectiveness of computer-based learning in meeting the professional development needs of teachers and schools, some more profound and underlying issues were highlighted. Positive indications regarding the potential value of computer-based multimedia in promoting development were obtained.

19. A project's model of change and manner of implementation strongly influenced the nature of the outcomes and the success with which they were achieved. The CLASS project targeted schools that appeared to possess the organisational qualities likely to benefit from multimedia independent learning systems on computerised management information systems. This model depends on the external agency having sufficient influence to draw schools into the project and to supply significant levels of resource and support without cost to the school. In the case of TML, the LEA support services took the view that they needed to offer something to all schools in the authority, in line with other initiatives in this area. As a result, they relied on schools opting in to the project and allocating their own resources to it. This 'thin layer' approach ensures equal access to new technology, but cannot have the same degree of impact on any one school as the targeted model favoured by CLASS.

20. Implementation seems likely to be more effective when a centrally-funded agency, with a recognised relevant expertise and track record, constructs a developmental strategy based upon prior analysis of school needs. A schedule of deliverable

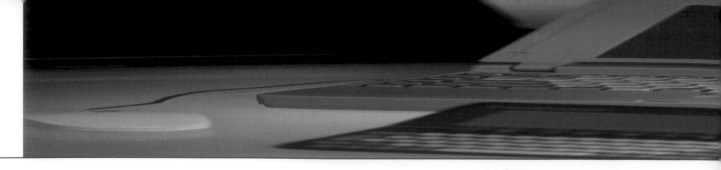

outcomes, with schools working in partnership with capable commercial and professional organisations that identify clear and feasible expectations of each other's achievement, is then more likely to succeed.

21. The CLASS project offers an interesting model for ICT-supported individualised learning as an effective means of providing 'point of need' professional development for teachers. This contrasts with the TML model, where one-off sessions were offered to schools on prescribed dates, with no prior knowledge of the state of readiness of the school or the availability of its staff.

22. In the case of use of ICT for curriculum-related work, it seems that schools who have already established an outward-looking approach to resourcing the curriculum are more likely to embrace superhighways technologies to enhance and extend this activity.

23. Each teacher in the CLASS project preferred the encountered school-based, independent learning model to a traditional centre-based model. There were several significant reasons given to substantiate this preference, which appeared to fit within the two categories of 'individual' and 'organisational'.

24. The CLASS change strategy appeared to promote effective change by adopting a 'pressure and support' hypothesis, whereby both the individual and the whole staff in schools are stimulated and sustained in 'change' activities by a combination of internal and external pressures and forms of support.

25. Programme design must quickly stimulate motivational factors. As the intrinsic value of the training

programme becomes apparent, the pressure mechanisms may reduce considerably. If, however, the support systems are reduced, motivation declines.

Administrative issues

26. Most secondary and many primary schools in the UK have some form of CMIS to assist with education administration. Supported by a pupil database, the system of integrated modules is able to automate a wide range of school administrative tasks, such as pupil and teacher records, assessment records, examination entries, pupil profiling, curriculum modelling and financial accounting. In addition, the system will also include generic software, such as word processing and spreadsheets, suitable for supporting both office administration and teachers' needs.

27. The impact of CMIS on a school's administrative teacher-support needs depends, in the main, upon the quality of forward planning the school itself makes for the introduction of the system, and the frequency with which the system is used. In the best possible cases, where the school engages in systematic advanced training and planned integration, co-ordinated by a school information management officer, schools have reported considerable benefits from CMIS. These benefits include the streamlining of office procedures, improvement in efficiency, speed and accuracy of administrative routines; reduction in clerical staff time, forestalling the need to appoint additional clerical staff; the delegation of routine administrative tasks from teachers to office and ancillary staff; improved financial monitoring and budgeting procedures; designing, costing, producing and distributing the school timetable; and reduction in the cost of producing information

and statistical returns for external bodies. In most instances, CMIS has enabled the school to meet its original administrative demands but it has also allowed the school to carry out new tasks, such as providing each pupil with a printed personal timetable.

28. The Cambridgeshire bulletin board project, which ran in parallel with the TML project but was not part of the EDSI evaluation, provided all schools in the LEA with an ICT channel for exchange of information between the CMIS and the LEA, as well as general dissemination of information relating to LEA support services, such as INSET course provision. This is an example of the strategic role that narrowband communications can play in school administration.

29. CMIS systems are large and complex integrated software applications, requiring significant staff development to realise their potential. The CLASS project offered an effective model for such professional development using video conferencing to support the use of an interactive CD-ROM based self-study training programme. This skills-and-knowledge based training, an important element of teachers' professional development, formed an essential first step in the eventual implementation of the CMIS. The ultimate objective is to improve school effectiveness, in terms of both school administration and education management, through improved decision making based on better information provision via the CMIS. However, as all those involved in education change realise, the transition from knowledge and skills acquisition to the implementation of sustainable change in school practices is complex and by no means guaranteed. It usually requires further support and training.

This next stage of the CLASS project, by necessity, will take place beyond the time-scale of the FDSI evaluation.

Project administration

30. The CLASS and TML projects offer an interesting contrast between what may be termed 'hot-spot' and 'broad-based' school development. Both projects were conceived and managed by local government agencies. In CLASS, the agency, assisted by significant investment from commercial and public partners, invested human and capital resources in a small number of targeted schools. In TML, the agency was concerned to raise the level of awareness across the LEA in some 300 schools. Key school personnel were targeted in each school, irrespective of the state of readiness of the school. It proved impossible to attract the level of sponsorship that would be required to make a significant impact on services, hardware or software provision to such a large number of schools. Furthermore, the schools themselves reported that they did not have sufficient funds available from existing budgets to support the installation or use of broadband ICT, or the necessary professional development required.

31. Both projects illustrate the ability of local government agencies to provide the professional development that schools require for effective ICT use. However, their ability to provide equality of access to such support for all schools will ultimately rest on the availability of funding for services, hardware, software and training, and effective targeting of those resources. Existing school funds will always be insufficient to meet all competing demands. Under local management of schools (LMS), local government agencies can only advise on the school development

agenda. If schools are to meet the current demands for implementation of ICT, they will need a clear message from Government that this is an imperative. This raises the need for an open debate on the value and appropriateness of ear-marked funding for ICT and associated professional development of teachers.

Implications

32. For successful school-based development, timing and reception conditions for the introduction of the training programme are crucial. It is possible, with due caution, to identify certain key characteristics that appear to be correlated with the successful application of multimedia-based independent learning programmes for purposes of individual professional and organisational development. There are a number of suggestions regarding the design and delivery of this professional development model on a wider basis that are likely to improve the chances of a successful outcome:

- prior needs analysis underpins the training programme

- an effective technical support system is available, with high-quality technical and advisory support provided

- a video-conferencing system is on line to provide help, and the remote tutor engages the learner in developmental questions leading to actual school uses

- multimedia learning systems need to be robust, user friendly and highly interactive, with practical content

- a video-conferencing system is used to test teachers on acquired skills, and the test results are used for the accreditation of teachers

- the teachers' professional

development should be managed at school level, with attention paid to auditing and supporting individuals

- the staff development structure is actively supported by the headteacher and co-ordinated by a senior member of staff

- staff development time is allocated to individual teachers

- the school allocates an appropriate, dedicated learning environment

- training is perceived as directly linked to school improvement.

Group D
Home-School Links
Executive Summary

The Projects

1. The three projects within this evaluation group were selected because they were, to greater or lesser extents, concerned with the use of communication technologies in the development of home-school links. Each project has been uniquely different with regard to its focus: one has been a largely technological trial with opportunistic educational development; another has been an ambitious development involving the width of aspects that need to be addressed in developing a learning community; the third has been a largely resource-based trial. One of the projects has directly supported the development of home-school practice, one was involved in the trial of a sophisticated technology within homes and schools, and the third was involved in educational trials of resources that could become available to homes as well as being used in schools.

Project D2.1: Acorn Home-School Links Project

Description of the project

2. This project involved eight primary schools (one of which later withdrew owing to a priority to prepare for an OFSTED inspection), two secondary schools, a college of higher education, and 92 homes (33 with children of school age). All sites were within the city of Cambridge, and all schools were in the Cambridge Local Education Authority (LEA).

3. The project lead sponsor was Acorn Online (originally Online Media). Other partners involved in creating the technological structure were Cambridge Cable, ATM Ltd, SJ Research and ICL. Partners involved in creating the resource provision were the BBC, Anglia Multimedia, Channel 4, the National Oracy Project (NOP), National Westminster Bank, Tesco and IPC Magazines.

4. The resources available, programmes located on large video servers, were accessed by users through a normal TV running a device that enabled them to select a programme on demand, through a set-top box, controlled by an infra-red panel. The programmes ran through a sophisticated asynchronous transfer mode (ATM) cable system. In one school, a large server and authoring centre were established in order to develop educational resources for use on the system.

5. The focus of the activity was twofold. Firstly, schools and homes used the technology, and considered educational uses for the system. Secondly, two particular sites were developed as authoring centres, and produced resources for wider access.

Aims and outcomes

6. The originally stated intentions for the project were that learners would be able to 'use IT in the home environment in close association with school work. Use on-line services in both home and school environment. Undertake work in the home environment that is structured and enabled by and through on-line services'. These intentions were largely not met; uses in homes and school have occurred independently, so aims and outcomes concerned with working between home and school in close association have not been fulfilled.

7. The outcomes from the project have indicated the ways in which homes and schools have used the technology and resources available, and how individual authoring sites have developed materials for use on the system. It is clear from the evaluation that school users of an iTV system require a great deal of training input if the resource is to be used in any more effective ways than a video and TV. It has been shown that it is possible for an experienced authoring centre to develop resources that link multimedia resources, video, audio, graphics and text, so that they are able to be run reliably over a sophisticated network. The use of such resources has not been demonstrated within the time-scale of this evaluation.

8. Professional development need was tackled largely in institutions by raising levels of awareness across the staff, and sharing ideas and experiences in either formal or informal ways. Awareness raising was offered by the lead sponsor at the start of the project, and technical support was available during the project. Teachers within schools generally required more development training than was available.

9. There were no reported influences on administration, whether at teacher, institution, or a wider level. Some teachers were able to propose ideas of how the systems could be used to support administration activities in the future.

10. In one school, visual display and repetition of material supported pupils with special educational needs.

Costs and cost benefits

11. For a school wishing to gain access to iTV, the costs are likely to be fairly low. Access to a cable system, costs associated with the provision of access to the resources, and the cost of a set-top box are the main costs involved. If a school wished to become an authoring centre, there are considerable costs involved in the technological provision required, such as servers, the time required to author resources, and the development of the expertise in order to undertake authoring of multimedia resources.

12. No cost benefits arose from schools involved in the project. However, the exposure of the authoring centre to national and international observers was high, and much interest was generated by those visiting.

Project D2.2: Highdown Information Hub Project

Description of the project

13. The lead school involved within this project is a comprehensive secondary school, and currently there are two other local secondary schools involved, as well as the Borough of Reading authority. There are 53 homes involved in the project, comprising 33 parents, 17 teachers, and three personnel from Reading Borough Council. All sites involved are currently within the borough and town of Reading.

14. The project lead sponsor has been Microsoft. Other technical sponsors have been ICL and Telecential. Training support has been provided by Softvision, and recently Inter Aid has agreed to provide support also. Resource support has been provided additionally by Superscape and Kodak.

15. The linking technology used has been based upon a cable system, with additional telephone links. The lead school has housed a 'hub', where resources are being developed, and accessed across the intranet within the school itself, within the other partner schools, and within the homes involved. Access is through standard PCs, using cable modems and, in some cases, telephone modems. The hub offers resource access to a range of specifically developed material, as well as to a range of Microsoft resources including CD-ROMs, and to the Internet.

16. The focus of the activity has been wide. The lead school and its partners have been involved in the management and development of the early stages of a learning community. The activity within the lead school has been to create a hub of useable resources; the activity within this school and the other linked schools and homes has been to use these resources for appropriate educational endeavour.

Aims and outcomes

17. The stated aims of the project were 'to demonstrate that the quality of education for young people and adults will be enhanced and value added by access to a well-organised information database made available through a broadband cable network'. While still at an early stage of development, the project has maintained its focus upon its aims and objectives, and within the time of this evaluation, the aims that could be reasonably expected to have been attained have been met.

18. The project has demonstrated that it has been possible, within the time-scale, to create a hub upon which a learning community could develop. Furthermore, it has demonstrated that management with a wide range of partners involved can lead to successful outcomes, where pupils in schools are gaining identifiable learning benefits, and where parents are also able to identify the benefits of the system. Pupil attainments have been shown to be enhanced in some cases by the uses of the resources, home involvement has been shown to have supported student learning, and pupils and parents have been shown to have been supported at home in educational endeavour by the system.

19. Professional development has been tackled within the project for teachers, pupils and parents. Creating involvement has been a key element within the professional development of all groups: teachers have been involved in both creating and using resources; pupils have been involved in classroom and home activities; and parents have been involved in resource identification and development, as well as use. Training has been tackled using a variety of means, including video support, awareness raising, and on-hand support.

20. Teachers are beginning to use the system to undertake class and school administrative tasks at home. The further use of the project is being discussed with Reading Borough Council, who plan to involve all their schools with links to the system. These would include links for administrative purposes.

21. Individual cases of educational outcomes for pupils with special educational needs at this time have not been identified. However, pupils with special educational needs have accessed the system readily, and resources have been identified that are appropriate for individuals. Examples of enhanced motivation arising from access and use have been reported.

Costs and cost benefits

22. A school wishing to develop as the centre of a hub would require a range of direct support in order to enable this to happen. The school involved has had a great deal of direct and indirect support from a wide range of sponsors. Without this support, the direct costs would be high. Costs would include those required to cover networking, computer hardware including servers, software, resource development, time to undertake management and development, and training. The school is within a newly

established unitary authority, and this creates the potential for the school and LEA to consider the ways in which hub developments relate to the likely needs of both institutions.

23. Schools involved in this project were able to gain significant benefits from access to the considerable experience and expertise of a wide range of personnel in industries and other schools. A range of parents have reported their greater involvement with the school and the education of their children. It is recognised by pupils, teachers and parents that the resources available through the project would have been difficult to gain in other ways, and that the access has provided cost benefit to them.

Project D2.3: Superhighways in Education Project

Description of the project

24. This project involved three secondary schools: two mixed comprehensive schools in Basildon, and a girls' grammar school in Maidstone. Recently six homes have become involved in the project.

25. The project's lead sponsor was Research Machines (RM). The other partner involved has been Telewest.

26. The resources available, remote CD-ROMs, Internet access, and cable TV channels, have been made available to the schools involved via the cable system through cable modems. The remote CD-ROMs have been held on a server in Basildon at Telewest, where cable TV channels have also originated. Originally, the Internet access was provided from RM, but the point of access has recently been moved to Telewest.

27. The focus of the activity has been the use of resources available via the cable system within learning activities in the schools involved.

Aims and outcomes

28. The stated aims of the project were 'to understand the likely eventual practicality and usefulness of educational systems developed using experimental broadband technology combined with existing school networks'. The central aim of the project was to consider the use of remote CD-ROM access and Internet access by secondary schools. So far, the use of remote CD-ROMs has been considered, and while there has been an overall lack of use in the schools, some sponsors are actively considering the possibility of providing access to remote CD-ROMs. The aims of the project have been met.

29. Educationally, a great deal has been learned about the management and use of these resources within schools, and within classrooms. Particularly, the means by which any school might gain access, and might need to develop use of the resources, has been highlighted by the experience of the schools involved in this project. While sponsors have taken a non-interventionist approach, this has meant that lessons about the possibilities of situations where large amounts of support are not provided can be learned and considered for the future. Enhanced educational attainment has been identified in some cases where resources are used to support cognitive processes such as comparison, analysis and synthesis.

30. Sponsors have been responsive to the technical needs of the schools involved, and have also supported the schools in their own professional development training. Awareness

raising, hands-on sessions, and paired development within departments have been the key ways in which schools have tackled their needs. Increasingly, more departments and more teachers have become involved in the use of resources in the schools.

31. The project did not in any school focus upon the administrative use of resources, but upon curriculum use. However, two of the schools are becoming more widely involved in the use of administrative packages to support teachers and pupils.

32. There were no notable outcomes associated with pupils with special educational needs, but teachers are indicating that pupils with particular needs are able to access the resources as readily as others. The need for appropriate language levels for pupils with special needs has been identified by a range of teachers involved.

Costs and cost benefits

33. The costs associated with undertaking a development of this type are concerned mainly with the development of an appropriate physical network within the school; the connection and access to resources via a cable or other link; the software required to access the resources; the deployment of appropriate levels of computer equipment in appropriate areas; staff development and training; maintenance and upgrading of equipment; and time for teachers or support staff to identify useable resources and the ways in which they might be used.

34. Staff within schools were able to gain access to expertise and support from personnel external to the school. It is recognised that the access has provided additional resources for the school, which could not have been either gained or funded in any other ways.

Cross-Project Observations and Recommendations

Teaching and learning issues

35. The resources used to the greatest extents within these projects have been Internet-based resources and e-mail.

36. Teachers judge the usefulness and useability of resources in a number of ways. However, access to resources is no substitute for the need for teachers to be creative in their approaches and uses of such resources. Where educational benefits have been identified, teachers are using on-line resources alongside others in integrated ways, rather than using them as a substitute for other resources, or as glorified worksheets.

37. Effective learning outcomes and improved attainments are reported and identifiable in some teaching and learning situations, and some uses are pointing towards some significant potential shifts within teaching and learning. Increased attainment is associated with the use of resources available via communication technologies to enhance cognitive learning processes such as integration of ideas, comparative analysis, reasoning and synthesis.

The technologies used

38. All projects have used a cable network for access to resources, but one has used a sophisticated ATM cable access.

39. There have been two main forms of resource used in the projects: programmes that run in sequential form, such as broadcast TV and radio programmes on demand; and resources that can be manipulated, such as Internet-related resources and CD-ROMs. The Internet has provided access to materials from three main sources: business, commerce and industry, the academic community (very largely in higher education); and individuals and groups concerned with a particular social focus (which includes pornographic material, and ways of restricting access to it). While teachers use these resources in many instances creatively and effectively, limited availability of material developed specifically for primary and secondary education is reported widely, both via iTV and the Internet.

Access and equity

40. To provide access for all to communication technologies, and to the resources they offer, will be likely to incur considerable costs. The least expensive means of those evaluated in these projects would be through an iTV route, but this provision could severely limit the ways in which resources could be manipulated by users, for example not having the facility to print off material. While equity of access is an important point to consider, and while libraries and community areas clearly have a role to play in helping to address such issues, as, indeed, could schools themselves, equity of use should be considered alongside this. Equity of provision of access will not automatically ensure equity of provision of use. It will be important that equity of access is coupled adequately with support, if use in particular or appropriate ways is to be a desirable outcome.

Project management and wider human networks

41. Many teachers are enthusiastic about projects of this type, but, in a climate where enthusiasm is generated, disillusionment can occur if concerns and problems are not managed appropriately.

42. Formidable obstacles have often been overcome in managing the development of these projects, and the significant time invested by those involved has led to beneficial outcomes when the partnership between public and private sector interests has been considered. Where successful outcomes have been identified, the management and development of three successive networks has been considered: the human network of partners and potential users; the physical network on which the human network will interact; and the resource network to be used by interested groups and parties concerned.

Partnerships between industry and educational institutions

43. Commitment from both industrial sponsors and staff within schools has been extremely high, and the EDSI projects within this evaluation can be considered to have met one of the intended objectives of encouraging companies to test new communications technology applications and their associated economics in the home-school context.

44. The type of involvement of schools has varied across projects and within projects. One school has largely led one project, while others have been led by the companies involved. Two schools have authored significant material, while others have used resources that have been accessed directly.

45. Schools within the projects in this evaluation group have taken two different developmental stances to the opportunities provided: 'evolutionary involvement'; and 'revolutionary acceptance'. Those schools who have succeeded to the greatest extents have been those who have taken the initiative, and have become fully involved in

planning their own evolutionary development with their partners. Those schools who have been confronted by the need for 'revolutionary acceptance' have not succeeded to the greatest extent: indeed, they have appeared often to reject the opportunity, or have felt under-used or under-valued.

46. The self-sufficiency of projects at this stage varies. One project will require increased company participation if it is to succeed beyond the point currently reached; another will rely upon continued and developing partnerships; the last will depend largely upon continued individual school involvement.

Future directions for suppliers

47. Mass production of books on line is unlikely to lead to successful educational outcomes or positive benefits at this time. Using on-line resources as a means to access worksheets has not been shown to lead to positive learning gains.

48. Suppliers face the issue of defining exactly what it is that is being supplied: if it is resources, then these are likely to need to be led by user suggestion; if it is curriculum enhancement, then this is likely to need to be coupled with the means to address teacher support and development in order that embedded resources can be used appropriately.

49. Suppliers also face issues concerned with copyright, intellectual property rights (IPR) and licensing. Major issues of this nature will need to be resolved if materials and resources are to become available and useable for educational purposes.

Future directions for education services

50. The evaluation outcomes suggest that the position from which

education originates is likely to become more varied in the future. The fact that in one of these projects a school could become a central resource hub for an authority highlights the question of where educational provision will in the future be centred.

51. The status of education may be raised to increasing extents by the potential and outcomes of the developed use of communication technologies. The demands and expectations upon pupils and upon schools could become higher. This could lead to a perceived enhancement of the status of education, but clearly there are associated issues of what effects this might have upon pupils in the future. The fact that parents can become more involved in supporting their children at home, and can more directly contact teachers, and view what their children are or should be doing, raises issues about their role, the role of the child, and the perceptions that they have of education.

52. The sheer range of those who are likely to be potentially affected by the advent of use of resources via communication technologies is staggering. For example, architects and those who build or modify schools will need to take account of networking provision needs in all rooms; caretakers will need to consider the security of schools when they are potentially open over much longer periods of time; meal providers may well find that they are asked to provide breakfasts and evening meals as well as lunches; curriculum policy makers may well need to consider how to integrate new approaches into curriculum documentation; authors may well need to consider whether they produce materials that are designed for communication technology use

as well as in book form; parents might need to consider how they will provide support for their children when the timing of school activities becomes more varied.

53. The effects upon individual schools are likely to be markedly different over the next 10 years. Some schools will develop and use communication technologies widely; others will not be able to take advantage of such resources, for a variety of reasons. This is likely to create two main effects: a diversity across schools with regard to their uses and practices with communication technologies; and a series of issues and questions for those who have to manage and handle this diversity. Any concept of the 'national' school is likely to become blurred as diversity bites, in terms of how teachers approach teaching and learning, and in terms of how schools organise and structure themselves.

Costs and cost benefits

54. Costs involved for schools fall into a range of categories. Schools will need to consider the ways in which they wish to use the technologies, as well as the ways in which they might gain access to resources, to judge the most cost-effective solutions.

Implications for the curriculum, present and future

55. The outcomes reported in this document all rely upon early evidence gathering, collected at very early stages of use. While some outcomes are significant, they raise the need to consider carefully issues of sustainability and generalisability for projects.

56. Corporate knowledge has in the past been defined by a school, and by individual teachers. Teachers have

been aware of the corporate knowledge they have needed to handle and to view, and pupils have been aware of what corporate knowledge they have needed to acquire and demonstrate. The resources available via communication technologies are offering new ranges of non-corporate knowledge. This non-corporate knowledge is neither accounted for within the current curriculum, nor is it a feature that teachers in general have experience of handling.

57. The use of communication technologies is already creating a shift in those schools involved in this evaluation towards more project-based learning activities and experiences. The curriculum as currently created is not based upon a project-orientated approach, but upon a subject-content approach. If the use of communication technologies is to be developed more widely, either teachers will need to use their initiative and creativity to develop activities to suit these new resources, or the curriculum may need to be developed so that such activities are able to be viewed more readily through the requirements and advice made available to them.

Professional development

58. Schools will need to consider a range of issues with regard to the introduction of communication technologies within classrooms. Management support will be needed to create time, opportunity and access. These provisions will need to be integrated with appropriate levels and forms of staff training and development. Such training will need to cover operational practice, pedagogical and curriculum practice, and multimedia handling and authoring. The effectiveness of uses of communication technologies will

undoubtedly depend upon appropriate professional development targeted at particular groups, which addresses key needs and issues. The four groups likely to need particular professional development are:

- managers
- co-ordinators
- teachers
- those involved in providing INSET.

59. There are implications for teacher training, both in terms of initial teacher training and continuing professional development, to integrate appropriate practice into courses and training: the ways in which adoption of resource use requires shifts in teacher thinking; in the need for developing appropriate policy within school; the means to develop successful teaching; and the background needs for management.

Administrative applications at individual, school and local levels

60. Teachers who are beginning to use communication technologies at home are beginning to plan lessons, make lesson notes, and undertake curriculum, classroom and school administration at home. However, the time demands upon teachers can be large. The need to account for this time demand undertaken in places other than schools, may well need to be considered by those designating terms and conditions of employment, since these do not currently directly address this scenario.

Home and community use

61. Not only will schools need positive support from school management and senior staff to develop use in ways similar to the projects reported here, but they will also need to consider their needs in terms of the

individuals or groups to be involved with the wider communication networks they are developing, including parents and the community.

62. The projects reported here have approached home-school links in different ways, and have reached different stages with regard to their development and practice. Early evidence from one project indicates that there may be significant benefits for parents when they become linked, via communication technologies, to the school and other personnel. There are major implications for future and further developments in this direction, for parents, pupils, teachers, schools and policy makers.

63. Home-school links are not a new concept. Parent-teacher associations, parent helpers in schools, teacher tutors in homes, and homework for completion outside lesson and school times are not new ideas. What communication technologies offer to the home-school link dimension is the development of new practice, the practice of parental support, the practice of involvement, and the practice of delivery, to extents that have previously been more limited. Parents can now view at home what pupils should be doing, they can support their children in their educational endeavours, and they can enable the delivery of certain courses or elements of courses within the home environment. In particular, communication technologies bring educational support into the home and transport the educational support normally available in schools into the home, to enable some parents to become involved educationally, and to strengthen educational support for their children to greater extents.

Special educational needs

64. Within this group of evaluations, the use of communication technologies to support pupils with special educational needs has not been high. However, some particular uses have been identified, for example where repetition of material and the highlighting of material through visual means can support pupils with particular needs. Also, teachers have recognised that while pupils with special educational needs may need material appropriate to their language skills, they have not appeared to have had any difficulty in accessing the systems and resources. Some schools are considering the ways in which communication technologies can support the delivery of the curriculum to pupils who have particular medical or physical problems.

Group E
Higher and Professional Education
Executive Summary

Project E2.1: Live-Links Project for Surgical Training

Description of the project

1. The focus of this report is on the use of live television links between an operating theatre in a regional hospital and the central teaching establishment in London at the Royal College of Surgeons. The live links at the college consist of a fibre-optic line to the Royal London Hospital and a dial-up 2Mbps Mercury Switchband link to four other hospitals. The system provides one-way video and two-way audio into three rooms in the college. Two are teaching rooms, holding 30–40 people, and the third is a large lecture room, seating up to 300.

2. The technology is used as part of training courses, usually on 'keyhole' surgery, for novice, intermediate and experienced surgeons.

Aims and outcomes

3. The aims of the project were to provide:
   - insights into the clinical applications of skills being learned during the courses by means of simulations, thus assisting in the transition from simulation into clinical practice
   - access to specialist teaching for a higher number of trainees
   - enhanced learning from the opportunity for participants at all levels to interact with the operating surgeon
   - better views of operative techniques than are frequently available locally
   - Master Classes where experts can present advances to their peers
   - minimal disruption to the clinical environment.

4. The results of the evaluation show that these aims have been largely met:
   - the technology is robust, appropriate and well supported
   - the educational value of the application of the technology is confirmed by trainees, tutors and the college
   - the system has raised the profile of the Royal College of Surgeons as a leading educational provider in surgical education.

Training

5. Although the college does believe that there is a need for formal 'teacher training' for more effective use of the technology, the current lack of such training does not seem to have a detrimental effect on the performance of teachers and learners at this level.

Funding

6. The start-up costs of the project, including five years rental of the fibre-optic line, were approximately £200,000 with running costs of £41.40 + VAT per half-hour for the Switchband link and £2,000 pa for the Mercury Switchband link rental. Grants were received for the set-up while running costs are met from course fees. The margins are very tight. There is no offsetting reduction in costs elsewhere to the college. It is an additional service. The system now runs on fees generated from courses. There are limits to the pricing the market will bear which allows the college little room for manoeuvre in terms of development of the system or integration of further hospital sites. Opportunity costs are to the surgeon tutors who offer their time free of charge.

Administration

7. The system does not put any organisational or cost burden on any agency other than the college. There are currently insufficient staff to use the material generated from live-links sessions to produce other educational materials such as videos and CD-ROMs. There is also some controversy about what type of material it would be best to produce.

Commercial relationships

8. Relationships with commercial companies have been less than satisfactory, experiencing difficulties in customer support, liaison, charging strategies and development work. Poor commercial relationships have limited the potential for international use of the system.

Technical functioning

9. Technical functioning of the system in use has been almost without problems. The system is unobtrusive and fulfils its functions well. The primary learning opportunity provided by the technology is the observation of experts at work: how they perform new techniques, how they handle difficulties and how they carry out various details of surgical operations.

Ethico-legal issues

10. Issues of copyright, confidentiality, danger to the patient and the responsibility of the observer for the safety of the operation are being addressed.

Educational value

11. There was a range of valuable teaching and learning outcomes:
   - The primary value of the particular application designed by the college is the interaction provided with the operating surgeon and the discussions fostered by the moderator, course tutors and trainees.
   - Trainees all endorsed the live-links programme. Watching a full operation in comfort, being able to discuss it and often having a

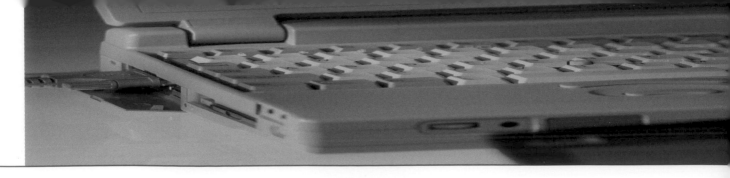

better view than presence in the operating theatre itself would afford, were very positively regarded.

- Integration of the live links with other educational events, such as simulated clinical practice and discussion, was a great strength. Watching an entire operation rather than edited highlights on video was appreciated, especially if the operating surgeon met with and solved unexpected problems.

- The system has solved the problem of how best to bring clinical material into the college for courses by offering access to the practice of a variety of surgeons, and the consequent opportunity for comparison of surgical techniques.

Coherence with existing surgical education

12. The new system enhances rather than replaces current practices:

- The value of the live-links learning was generally seen to be in the speeding up of practical learning when the participants eventually returned to the operating theatre. It was predicted that gains would be made in the actual amount of clinical contact time required to reach mastery of a procedure. This has yet to be proved but is a common hypothesis.

- The technology fits in with and builds on the existing effective ways of learning surgery and with the professional culture associated with that.

- It avoids competing pressures on the participants' time by removing them from their site of practice.

- It is, essentially, a support rather than a change of direction or free-standing innovation.

- The benefits of the technology are in its capacity to make available to a varied audience experience and knowledge which would otherwise be more time-consuming and difficult to acquire. The technology received almost total endorsement from those who had used it.

Options for expansion

13. Given the availability of funding, a variety of options for expansion were reviewed including:

- making videotapes of the live-links material for sale to other hospitals and educators

- expansion to further hospital sites

- broadcasting of other kinds of surgical procedure

- extending the audience to other doctors and paramedical specialties

- multipointing

- integration with other technologies, such as the virtual microscope and the World Wide Web.

Group F
Additional Projects
Executive Summary

The Projects

The following reports are based on the findings of three projects which were not part of the original EDSI submission, but are wholly funded and administered by Government Departments and agencies. Each brings a unique perspective to the use of the superhighways which is not replicated by other EDSI projects, and therefore provides a broader picture.

The three additional projects and their unique features are:

- *the Educational Internet Service Providers project, which explores the effect of networked access to the Internet for teaching and learning*

- *Lingu@NET – a virtual language centre, which explores the development of a World Wide Web site for language teachers*

- *the Multimedia Portables for Teachers Pilot, which has provided individual teachers with portable computing facilities, including access to the Internet and e-mail.*

Because the starting dates of these three projects were different from the main EDSI projects, only interim reports are available at this stage.

Project F2.1: Educational Internet Service Providers Project

Description of the project

1. The aim of the Educational Internet Service Providers project (EISP) is to investigate the curriculum benefits of Internet service providers and the effect on teaching and learning of networked access to the Internet. The project is funded by the Department for Education and Employment (DfEE) and is administered by the National Council for Educational Technology (NCET). Additional support is provided by Dialnet and RM Internet for Learning in the form of some initial free access to the Internet. The project currently involves over 350 schools.

2. Four 'core schools' were selected on a bid basis to receive equipment and resources to the value of over £35,000 per school to establish a distributed Internet network. This 'core' comprises two secondary schools, one primary school and a special school. Conditions of the bidding process included a requirement that each school provided £10,000 per year from its own resources and showed in its development plans a commitment to information and communications technology (ICT). They were provided with a basic network cabling infrastructure and ISDN2 Internet connection, a router, a file server and a number of multimedia computer systems, either Research Machines (RM) or Acorn, together with a range of curriculum-related software. The schools spent additional funding where they required additional cabling or wished to connect additional computers. The Internet service is provided by either RM or Dialnet.

3. Fifty 'focus schools' are taking part in the project, representing a range of geographical locations, types of installation and types of school, in order to make comparisons between:
   - stand-alone Internet access and networked access
   - styles of classroom management
   - effects on learning
   - management and technical issues associated with connectivity.

4. Half of these schools are in the primary age range, including four middle schools, four are special schools and the rest are a range of different types of secondary school located across the country.

5. Towards the end of the project, approximately 300 'volunteer schools' will be completing a questionnaire on their use and perceptions of the Internet for teaching and learning.

6. Professional development was undertaken by the service providers in the first instance and also by the NCET project officer. The nature of the training has moved from being very general and technical to being targeted at particular curriculum needs. Demand for training is continuing throughout the project.

Aims and outcomes

7. The project aims to evaluate:
   - the impact of Internet access on learning
   - the value of specific educational Internet services currently on offer to schools
   - the impact of Internet access on management and administration both in the classroom and in the whole school
   - how technical issues affect the process of learning.

8. The NCET project officer has provided training and supported staff at the four core schools. This has included curriculum areas, technical matters, Web site creation, searching effectively, e-mail and newsgroups. A mailing list has been set up to which any schools using the Internet may subscribe.

9. Early indications are that the Internet is being used in five ways:
   - personal search by pupils
   - integration of Web materials into teaching
   - tasks based on Web searches
   - Web page creation
   - communication.

Costs and cost benefits

10. The core schools are being asked to provide a breakdown of these and details will appear in the final report together with case studies and a detailed evaluation of the project.

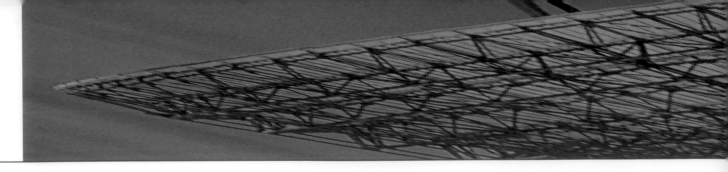

Project F2.2: Lingu@NET - A Virtual Language Centre

Description of the project

11. Lingu@NET is a UK developmental project led by two Government-funded organisations, the National Council for Educational Technology and the Centre for Information on Language Teaching and Research (CILT), to develop a Web site of quality-assured resources for language teachers. Its address is www.ncet.org.uk/linguanet. The Lingu@NET project began in January 1996 and currently runs until December 1998. European funding is being sought to continue the project until 2000. The project and the budget are managed by NCET, who report to a steering group consisting of representatives of DfEE, CILT and NCET. NCET and CILT jointly design and structure the site, define the criteria for inclusion of materials, and promote the site.

Aims and outcomes

12. The aim is to establish a Web-based language centre, based on networked information technology, providing UK language teachers with quality-assured information, INSET materials and expert advice. The objectives of the project are to:

    - test the concept of an on-line education support centre as a replicable model

    - provide material for education professionals, related to the teaching and learning of languages on a Web site

    - obtain evidence relating to networking, quality control, user needs and commercial opportunities

    - set up a high-performance Sun Netra server.

13. Since Lingu@NET is a developmental project, there is no formal evaluation element.

14. The project has met its four aims, in some respects exceeding them:

    - The site contains over 50 documents not available elsewhere and has links to over 150 other sites. The documents include those in English, French, German, Spanish and Welsh.

    - The site includes an on-line enquiry service and opportunities for feedback. By December 1997, there will be a discussion group and more links to materials supporting professional dialogue.

    - Through the on-line feedback form, reports from the user groups, discussions with CILT and publishers and those experienced in setting up the server, there is now a clearer picture of what language teachers want from the Internet, an understanding of commercial and quality-assurance issues in a new medium and a deeper appreciation of server and connectivity issues.

    - The Sun Netra server is now running and performing to specification. A secure transaction system is expected to go live in 1997.

15. The following outcomes have been achieved:

    - The Lingu@NET Web site is established on a high-performance server.

    - A network of formal and informal user groups has been set up.

    - Partnerships are in place between government-funded organisations, the public and private sectors, providers and users, and the UK and other countries.

    - There is considerable interest among publishers, and NCET and CILT have assisted them in going on line and reaching a market outside the UK.

    - Further evidence has been gathered of how the Internet is truly a global phenomenon, with implications for how the UK education service functions.

    - Evidence suggests that the use of Lingu@NET by teachers for their own professional purposes may well provoke change in their attitude to and use of ICT in classrooms, for example by helping learners to develop the information-handling skills they need to access language-related support materials.

    - Lingu@NET works for language teachers. There is no reason why the concept could not work in other curriculum areas. The potential of on-line professional support is vast. There is much more to do, notably in the areas of peer-to-peer networking, for example by SENCOs, teachers as publishers, and through on-line tutorials and international partnerships.

Sponsors and other partners

16. The project was 100% funded to March 1997 by the DfEE. Other parties, in addition to NCET and CILT, include commercial publishers and international partners in G7 and other countries. Over 200 different users visit the site every week, using the full range of connectivity. The project is funding user groups who have contributed materials and ideas and are developing innovative practices.

Costs and cost benefits

17. Lingu@NET is only as far away as a telephone line. Users in Cornwall, Lancaster and Wales are not disadvantaged by the distance to CILT and NCET as they are if they need to travel to a conference or exhibition. The quality and authority of the materials is not reduced if the school lacks local guidance or expertise in languages.

18. Everything on the site is free of charge to the user. Since there is no training or support element, there are no additional costs as more people access the resources and so the more accesses, the more cost-effective. Whether people would pay to access Lingu@NET is yet to be determined; the resources offered would be free of charge if obtained from NCET, CILT, the Association for Language Learning (ALL) or if collected at an exhibition, but on-line access is more convenient and has fewer travel or time overheads.

19. Where Lingu@NET really begins to save travel time, then the money saved could be moved into equipment and access provision both in school and at home. However, a visit to a virtual language centre and publishers' exhibition can, of course, never recreate the bonds forged at a real event.

20. Lingu@NET uses standard Internet tools and norms; it has no proprietary features or requirements. This is particularly important for novice and overseas users. The site (as with others in English) should welcome people and explain itself in other languages, as is the practice on non-English sites.

21. As a means of national organisations reaching their target audience, Lingu@net would be cost-effective if more teachers were on line. The on-costs of preparing a page of information are about £40 and that page can be seen by thousands of people.

22. Lingu@NET could be commercially viable if it could bring customers to product suppliers, generate its own income through product sales, or enable existing funding of an organisation's work to be redirected, for example from a telephone/letter enquiry service to an on-line information-provision service and thereby to more efficient ways of working.

Project F2.3: Multimedia Portables for Teachers Pilot

Description of the project

23. The Multimedia Portables for Teachers Pilot is a project to investigate how the provision of high-quality portable computers with software and Internet access could support the development of teacher confidence and competence in the use of IT.

24. The project was funded solely by the DfEE and has two phases. In Phase I, there were approximately 1,150 teachers in 65 primary, 24 middle, 462 secondary and 16 special schools involved in the project, distributed pro rata in each of the English local education authorities and the grant-maintained sector. Every school had two teachers working on the project, each with their own machine. The evaluation of Phase I is complete.

25. This pilot has been extended into a second phase with a further 390 teachers. Phase II runs from January 1997 to July 1998.

Aims and outcomes

26. The aims of the initiative are to:
    - provide a varied group of teachers with personal computers that support multimedia and/or communications
    - increase teacher confidence and competence in the use of ICT resources
    - promote better learning in the pupils taught by the teachers taking part in the pilot.

27. The evaluators found that teacher competence has significantly increased with high figures for successful usage in all areas of the technology provided. Over 98% of teachers made successful use of the computers, over 90% of teachers made successful use of CD-ROM and 76% made successful use of the Internet. In addition, 95% of the teachers used the computers at school for teaching purposes and 90% for administrative activities.

28. Evidence showed that 99% of teachers used the computer at home to complete work started at school, and it was apparent that for most teachers the equipment had become fully integrated into their professional lives.

29. Improved confidence was identified in both the statistical and the case-study evidence, with teachers feeling they had increased their knowledge of IT substantially and that the project had provided positive benefits for teaching and learning.

30. NCET, who managed the project on behalf of the DfEE, considers that four main conditions contributed to the success of the pilot:
    - initial and immediate success with the technology
    - personal ownership and exclusive use of the computer over an extended period
    - the portability of the equipment, which enabled it to be moved between work areas and between home and school
    - formal and informal support were required, and the combination of ownership and portability provided teachers with the flexibility to access a great variety of support from peers and other sources.

31. The final report will be published shortly.

Costs

32. The cost of the equipment provision was approximately £5 million. This provided a total of some 1,500 machines, in two phases, with personal productivity software and a selection of CD-ROMs and Internet-access accounts. A three-hour on-site demonstration was also provided as part of the funding. The market cost of each package, including hardware, software, Internet access and demonstration, would be in excess of £4,000 for Phase I of the project, although this price is falling substantially.

33. The independent evaluation was carried out by a team led by Professor Colin Harrison from the University of Nottingham. The evaluation used quantitative and qualitative data gathered between June 1996 and May 1997 and included detailed statistical and case-study analysis.